A Yuletide Treasury of
POEMS, CAROLS
AND SONGS

A Yuletide Treasury of
POEMS, CAROLS
AND SONGS

Words that Celebrate the Season
EDITED BY SARAH ANNE STUART

BRISTOL
PARK
BOOKS

PUBLISHER'S NOTE

This collection of poems, carols and songs contain historic styles of spelling
and punctuation, as well as words expressing the language of earlier times.
The original texts have been reproduced exactly as written to maintain the
integrity of the words. We hope the modern reader will view these works
within the context of their time period.

The Acknowledgements on pages 313 to 315 constitute an extension
of the copyright page.

First Bristol Park Books paperback edition published in 2012

Bristol Park Books
252 W. 38th Street
NYC, NY 10018

Bristol Park Books is a registered trademark of Bristol Park Books, Inc.
Library of Congress Control Number: 2011930433
ISBN: 978-0-88486-498-1

Text and jacket designed by LaBreacht Design

Printed in the United States of America

Contents

Introduction SARAH ANNE STUART xi

THE GIFT OF HOPE

O Come, O Come, Emmanuel TRADITIONAL FRENCH CAROL 3
Come, Thou Long-Expected Jesus CHARLES WESLEY 6
Lo, How a Rose E'er Blooming TRADITIONAL GERMAN CAROL 7
Christmas Bells ALFRED, LORD TENNYSON 8
Christmas Eve JOHN DRINKWATER 10
Christmas WILLIAM CULLEN BRYANT 12
The Light of Bethlehem JOHN BANNISTER TABB 13
Once In Royal David's City MRS. CECIL FRANCES ALEXANDER 14
The Nativity G.K. CHESTERTON 16
Saint Stephen and King Herod AUTHOR UNKNOWN 19
The Oxen THOMAS HARDY 22
It Came Upon the Midnight Clear EDMUND HAMILTON SEARS 23

THE BLESSED JOURNEY

The Cherry Tree Carol TRADITIONAL ENGLISH CAROL 27
As Joseph Was A-Walking AUTHOR UNKNOWN 29
Coventry Carol ROBERT CROO 31
The House of Christmas G.K. CHESTERTON 32
How Far Is It to Bethlehem FRANCES CHESTERTON 34
The Barn ELIZABETH COATSWORTH 36

The Stable GABRIELA MISTRAL 38
O Little Town of Bethlehem PHILLIPS BROOKS 40
A Christmas Folk-Song LISETTE WOODWORTH REESE 42
Christmas Carol MAY PROBYN 43
The Seven Joys of Mary TRADITIONAL ENGLISH CAROL 46
The Peaceful Night JOHN MILTON 49
A Christmas Carol G.K. CHESTERTON 51
Christmas Carol SARA TEASDALE 52

THE GUIDING STAR

As I Sat Under a Sycamore Tree AUTHOR UNKNOWN 57
I Saw Three Ships AUTHOR UNKNOWN 59
The Three Ships ALFRED NOYES 61
Carol of the Brown King LANGSTON HUGHES 64
The Kings of the East KATHERINE LEE BATES 66
Three Kings of Orient JOHN HENRY HOPKINS 68
Ballad of the Epiphany CHARLES DALMON 71
The Three Kings HENRY WADSWORTH LONGFELLOW 74

COME LET US ADORE HIM

Before the Paling of the Stars CHRISTINA ROSSETTI 81
Christus Natus Est COUNTEE CULLEN 83
A Christmas Hymn RICHARD WATSON GILDER 85
A Hymn for Christmas Day THOMAS CHATTERTON 87
Hark! The Herald Angels Sing CHARLES WESLEY 90
Whence Comes This Rush of Wings? TRADITIONAL FRENCH CAROL 92
O Come, All Ye Faithful FREDERICK OAKLEY 93
A Child This Day Is Born TRADITIONAL ENGLISH CAROL 96
While Shepherds Watched Their Flocks By Night NAHUM TATE 99

What Child Is This? WILLIAM CHATTERTON DIX...............................101

Angels We Have Heard on High TRADITIONAL FRENCH CAROL 103

The Holy Night ELIZABETH BARRETT BROWNING.............................105

The First Nowell TRADITIONAL ENGLISH CAROL 106

Away In a Manger AUTHOR UNKNOWN 108

Angels from the Realms of Glory JAMES MONTGOMERY 110

O Holy Night JOHN SULLIVAN DWIGHT.....................................112

Psalm for Christmas Day THOMAS PESTEL..................................114

New Prince, New Pomp ROBERT SOUTHWELL..............................116

A Carol LISETTE WOODWORTH REESE 118

On the Morning of Christ's Nativity JOHN MILTON..........................119

A Christmas Carol CHRISTINA ROSSETTI...................................131

Christmas Morning ELIZABETH MADDOX ROBERTS...........................133

A Christmas Carol for Children MARTIN LUTHER...........................135

No Sweeter Thing ADELAIDE LOVE 137

Choir-Boys on Christmas Eve LOUISE TOWNSEND NICHOLL...................138

Good Christian Men, Rejoice TRADITIONAL GERMAN CAROL....................139

O Come Little Children JOHANN A.P. SCHULZ 141

Silent Night, Holy Night JOSEPH MOHR 142

The Priceless Gift of Christmas HELEN STEINER RICE..........................144

The Glory of Christmas LAVERNE RILEY O'BRIEN 146

Go Tell It on the Mountain TRADITIONAL AFRICAN-AMERICAN SPIRITUAL.........147

The Hallowed Season WILLIAM SHAKESPEARE 149

Carol of the Field Mice KENNETH GRAHAME................................150

Joy to the World ISAAC WATTS 152

THE MERRY SEASON

Hymn for Christmas Day JOHN BYROM......................................155

The Most Wonderful Time of the Year EDDIE POLA AND GEORGE WYLE..........158

Christmas Morning JOAQUIN MILLER...160

Christmas Everywhere PHILLIPS BROOKS 161

Christmas Snowflakes SASHA ISABELLA ALEXANDER 163

Deck the Halls TRADITIONAL WELSH CAROL............................164

The Holly and the Ivy TRADITIONAL ENGLISH CAROL...............166

Christmas Time Is Here LEE MENDELSON AND VINCE GUARALDI..................169

A Christmas Carol AUTHOR UNKNOWN..................................170

Now Is the Time of Cristmas JAMES RYMAN 171

The Love That Lives W.D. DORRITY......................................172

The Christmas Song (Chestnuts Roasting on An Open Fire)
       MEL TORME AND ROBERT WELLS.....................................173

Masters in This Hall WILLIAM MORRIS 174

Pat-A-Pan TRADITIONAL FRENCH CAROL..............................177

Merry Christmas LOUISA MAY ALCOTT.................................178

We Need a Little Christmas JERRY HERMAN 180

All You That to Feasting and Mirth Are Inclined AUTHOR UNKNOWN..........182

The Christmas Tree EMMA LAZARUS...................................183

Silver Bells JAY LIVINGSTON AND RAY EVANS........................186

God Rest You Merry, Gentlemen TRADITIONAL ENGLISH CAROL 188

Christ Was Born on Christmas Day TRADITIONAL GERMAN CAROL.............192

O Christmas Tree TRADITIONAL GERMAN CAROL....................193

I Am Cristmas JAMES RYMAN 195

Ceremonies for Candelmas ROBERT HERRICK......................197

Christmas Pie GEORGE WITHER 199

Christmas in a Village JOHN CLARE 200

Ceremonies for Christmasse ROBERT HERRICK....................203

Jingle Bells JAMES S. PIERPONT 205

little tree e.e. cummings 208

Christmas Laughter NIKKI GIOVANNI................................210

DEAR SANTA

The Boy Who Laughed at Santa Claus OGDEN NASH 215
Here Comes Santa Claus (Right Down Santa Clause Lane)
        GENE AUTRY AND OAKLEY HALDEMAN 219
Kris Kringle THOMAS BAILEY ALDRICH 221
Christmas Island KATHERINE LEE BATES 222
Santa's Stocking KATHERINE LEE BATES 226
Saint Nicholas MARIANNE MOORE 228
Jolly Old St. Nicholas TRADITIONAL AMERICAN CAROL 230
Santa Claus WALTER de la MARE 231
Santa Claus Is Comin' to Town HAVEN GILLESPIE AND J. FRED COOTS 233
A Visit from St. Nicholas CLEMENT C. MOORE 235

THE JOY OF GIVING

All the Days of Christmas PHYLLIS McGINLEY 241
It's Beginning to Look Like Christmas MEREDITH WILLSON 243
Karma EDWIN ARLINGTON ROBINSON 245
Christmas Carol PHILLIPS BROOKS 246
Good King Wenceslas JOHN M. NEALE 248
The Twelve Days of Christmas TRADITIONAL ENGLISH CAROL 250
Jest 'Fore Christmas EUGENE FIELD 255
A Friend's Greeting EDGAR A. GUEST 258
A Christmas List MARILYN MORGAN HELLEBERG 259
Scrooge Rides Again OGDEN NASH 261
Somehow JOHN GREENLEAF WHITTIER 265

CHRISTMAS MEMORIES

I Remember Yule OGDEN NASH 269
Christ Climbed Down LAWRENCE FERLINGHETTI 271

Christmas E. HILTON YOUNG 275
Noel: Christmas Eve, 1913 ROBERT BRIDGES 276
Christmas in the Olden Time SIR WALTER SCOTT 279
White Christmas IRVING BERLIN 284
Christmas Eve at Sea JOHN MASEFIELD 285
The Mahogany Tree WILLIAM MAKEPEACE THACKERAY 287
The Inexhaustibility of the Subject of Christmas LEIGH HUNT 290
I'll Be Home for Christmas WALTER KENT, KIM GANNON AND BUCK RAM 293
Christmas Bells HENRY WADSWORTH LONGFELLOW 294
Christmas at Sea ROBERT LOUIS STEVENSON 296
On Going Home for Christmas EDGAR A. GUEST 299

RING OUT THE OLD, RING IN THE NEW

Here We Come A-Wassailing TRADITIONAL ENGLISH CAROL 303
Christmas Greeting from a Fairy to a Child LEWIS CARROLL 306
We Wish You a Merry Christmas TRADITIONAL ENGLISH CAROL 308
Peace HENRY VAUGHAN 310
Auld Lang Syne ROBERT BURNS 311

ACKNOWLEDGMENTS 313
INDEX OF FIRST LINES. 319
INDEX OF POETS AND LYRICISTS 325
INDEX OF POEMS, CAROLS AND SONGS. 327

Introduction

SARAH ANNE STUART

FOR OVER TWO THOUSAND YEARS poets, writers, and lyricists have penned words to celebrate the season—the season of Christmas. *A Yuletide Treasury of Poems, Carols, and Songs* highlights the special meanings of Christmas, from the anticipation of the birth of the Savior, to the joy, love, giving, and sharing that we experience during this wonderful time of year.

Classic poems and carols, beginning with the traditional "O Come, O Come Emmanuel," tell the story of the babe who filled the world with light. The carols and poems, including "Silent Night, Holy Night," "Hark! the Herald Angels Sing," "Joy to the World," "Three Kings of Orient," and "The Priceless Gift of Christmas" are a tribute to the wondrous miracle of the child in Bethlehem born.

Christmas is truly a merry season celebrated with the lyrics of contemporary songs like "The Most Wonderful Time of the Year," "We Need a Little Christmas." the traditional carol, "Deck the Halls!" and the classic poem "The Twelve Days of Christmas."

And it is also a time for sharing special memories as echoed in the poems "On Going Home for Christmas," "Christmas at Sea," "I Remember Yule," and the classic lyrics of "White Christmas."

It is my hope that as you discover the riches contained in *A Yuletide Treasury of Poems, Carols, and Songs* you will make this volume a part of your Christmas traditions this year and for many years to come. As the season comes to and end, "We Wish You a Merry Christmas," "Peace on Earth, Good Will Toward Men," and leave you with "Auld Lang Syne."

Sarah Anne Stuart

A Yuletide Treasury of
POEMS, CAROLS
AND SONGS

The Gift of
HOPE

O Come, O Come Emmanuel

TRADITIONAL FRENCH CAROL

O come, O come, Emmanuel
And ransome captive Israel,
That mourns in lonely exile here
Until the Son of God appear.

Rejoice! Rejoice!
Emmanuel
Shall come to thee
O Israel.

O come, Desire of nations, bind
All people in one heart and mind;
Bid envy, strife, and quarrels cease;
Fill the whole world with heaven's peace.

Rejoice! Rejoice!
Emmanuel

Shall come to thee
O Israel.

O come, Thou Day-spring, come and cheer
Our spirits by Thine advent here;
Disperse the gloomy clouds of night,
And death's dark shadows put to flight.

Rejoice! Rejoice!
Emmanuel
Shall come to thee
O Israel.

O come, O come, Thou Rod of Jesse, free
Thine own from Satan's tyranny;
From depth of hell Thy people save,
And give them victory o'er the grave.

Rejoice! Rejoice!
Emmanuel
Shall come to thee
O Israel.

O come, Thou Key of David, come,
And open wide our heav'nly home;
Make safe the way that leads on high,
And close the path to misery.

Rejoice! Rejoice!
Emmanuel
Shall come to thee
O Israel.

O come, O come, Thou Lord of might,
Who once, from Sinai's flaming height
Didst give the trembling tribes Thy law,
In cloud, and majesty, and awe.

Rejoice! Rejoice!
Emmanuel
Shall come to thee
O Israel.

Come, Thou Long-Expected Jesus

CHARLES WESLEY

Come, thou long-expected Jesus,
　　Born to set thy people free;
From our fears and sins release us,
　　Let us find our rest in thee.

Israel's strength and consolation,
　　Hope of all the earth thou art;
Dear desire of every nation,
　　Joy of every longing heart.

Born thy people to deliver,
　　Born a child, and yet a king,
Born to reign in us for ever,
　　Now thy gracious kingdom bring.

By thine own eternal Spirit
　　Rule in all our hearts alone:
By thine all-sufficient merit
　　Raise us to thy glorious throne. Amen.

Lo, How a Rose E'er Blooming

TRADITIONAL GERMAN CAROL

Lo, how a Rose e'er blooming,
From tender stem has sprung!
Of Jesse's lineage coming,
As men of old have sung.
It came, a flow'ret bright,
Amid the cold of winter,
When half spent was the night.

Isaiah 'twas foretold it.
The rose I have in mind,
With Mary we behold it,
The Virgin Mother kind.
To show God's love aright,
She bore to men a Saviour,
When half-spent was the night.

Christmas Bells

ALFRED LORD TENNYSON

The time draws near the birth of Christ:
    The moon is hid; the night is still;
    The Christmas bells from hill to hill
Answer each other in the mist.

Four voices of four hamlets round,
    From far and near, on mead and moor,
    Swell out and fail, as if a door
Were shut between me and the sound:

Each voice four changes on the wind,
    That now dilate, and now decrease,
    Peace and goodwill, goodwill and peace,
Peace and goodwill, to all mankind.

This year I slept and woke with pain,
    I almost wish'd no more to wake,
    And that my hold on life would break
Before I heard those bells again:

But they my troubled spirit rule,
    For they controll'd me when a boy;
    They bring me sorrow touch'd with joy,
The merry merry bells of Yule.

Christmas Eve

JOHN DRINKWATER

On Christmas Eve I lay abed,
With the still night more still
For all the pluming snows that spread
Along our sparkling hill,
And while again to Jesu' stall
Walked wisdom from afar,
I heard another shepherd call
Under the Christmas star.

Along the lane his carol came,
But not of Bethlehem,
A burning boy, he knew a flame,
But not the flame of them:
"This Christmas Eve from courting home
I am a bachelor,
But soon the snows again will come,
And I'll be wed before."

All one with kinds from Bible-page
    And holy shepherds old,
Went yeoman love in pilgrimage
    Across the Christmas wold.
"Goodwill," he sang, "Goodwill, Goodwill,"
    Or seemed to me to sing,
While some glad girl beyond the hill
    Dreamt of a new-born king.

Christmas

WILLIAM CULLEN BRYANT

As shadows cast by cloud and sun
    Flit o'er the summer grass,
So, in Thy sight, Almighty One,
    Earth's generations pass.
And as the years, an endless host,
Come swiftly pressing on,
The brightest names that earth can boast
    Just glisten and are gone.

Yet doth the star of Bethlehem shed
    A lustre pure and sweet:
And still it leads, as once it led,
    To the Messiah's feet.
O Father, may that holy star
    Grow every year more bright,
And send its glorious beams afar
    To fill the world with light.

The Light of Bethlehem

JOHN BANISTER TABB

'Tis Christmas night! The snow,
    A flock unnumbered, lies:
The old Judean stars, aglow,
    Keep watch within the skies.

An icy stillness holds
    The pulses of the night:
A deeper mystery infolds
    The wondering hosts of light.

Till, lo, with reverence pale
    That dims each diadem,
The lordliest, earthward bending, hail
    The light of Bethlehem!

Once In Royal David's City

MRS. CECIL FRANCES ALEXANDER

Once in Royal David's city
Stood a lowly cattle shed,
Where a mother laid her baby
In a manger for his bed.
Mary was that mother mild
Jesus Christ her little child.

He came down to earth from heaven
Who is God and Lord of all,
And His shelter was a stable,
And His cradle was a stall.
With the poor and mean and lowly
Lived on earth our Savior holy.

And through all His wondrous childhood
He would honor and obey,
Love and watch the lowly maiden,

In whose gentle arms He lay.
Christian children all must be,
Mild, obedient, good as He.

For he is our childhood's pattern,
Day by day like us He grew,
He was little, weak and helpless,
Tears and smiles like us He knew,
And He feeleth for our sadness,
And He shareth in our gladness.

And our eyes at last shall see Him,
Through His own redeeming love,
For that Child so dear and gentle
Is our Lord in heaven above,
And He leads his children on
To the place where He is gone.

Not in that poor lowly stable,
With the oxen standing by,
We shall see Him, but in heaven
Set at God's right hand on high,
Where, like stars, His children crowned
All in white shall wait around.

The Nativity

G.K. CHESTERTON

The thatch on the roof was as golden,
Though dusty the straw was and old,
The wind had a peal as of trumpets,
Though blowing and barren and cold,
The mother's hair was a glory
Though loosened and torn,
For under the eaves in the gloaming
A child was born.

Have a myriad children been quickened,
Have a myriad children grown old,
Grown gross and unloved and embittered,
Grown cunning and savage and cold?
God abides in a terrible patience,
Unangered, unworn,
And again for the child that was squandered
A child is born.

What know we of aeons behind us,
Dim dynasties lost long ago,
Huge empires, like drams unremembered,
Huge cities for ages laid low?
This at least—that with blight and with blessing,
With flower and with thorn,
Love was there, and his cry was among them,
"A child is born."

Though the darkness be noisy with systems,
Dark fancies that fret and disprove,
Still the plumes stir around us, above us
The wings of the shadow of love:
Oh! Princes and priests, have ye seen it
Grow pale through your scorn;
Huge dawns sleep before us, deep changes,
A child is born.

And the rafters or toil still are gilded
With the dawn of the stars of the heart,
And the wise men draw near in the twilight,
Who are weary of learning and art,
And the face of the tyrant is darkened,
His spirit is torn,
For a new king is enthroned; yea, the sternest,
A child is born.

And the mother still joys for the whispered
First stir of unspeakable things,
Still feels that high moment unfurling
Red glory of Gabriel's wings.
Still the babe of an hour is a master
Whom angels adorn,
Emmanuel, prophet, anointed,
A child is born.

And thou, that art still in thy cradle,
The sun being crown for thy brow,
Make answer, our flesh, make an answer,
Say, whence art thou come—who art thou?
Art thou come back on the earth for our teaching
To train or to warn—?
Hush—how may we know?—knowing only
A child is born.

Saint Stephen
and King Herod

AUTHOR UNKNOWN

Saint Stephen was a clerk
  In King Herod's hall,
And servèd him of bread and cloth
  As ever king befall.

Stephen out of kitchen came,
  With boar's head on hand,
He saw a star was fair and bright
  Over Bethlehem stand.

He cast adown the boar's head
  And went into the hall:
"I forsake thee, King Herod,
  And thy workès all;

"I forsake thee, King Herod,
  And thy workès all;
There is a child in Bethlehem born
  Is better than we all."

"What aileth thee, Stephen?
  What is thee befall?
Lacketh thee either meat or drink
  In King Herod's hall?"

"Lacketh me neither meat nor drink
  In King Herod's hall;
There is a child in Bethlehem born
  Is better than we all."

"What aileth thee, Stephen?
  Art thou wode or ginnest to breed?
Lacketh thee either gold or fee
  Or any rich weed?"

"Lacketh me neither gold nor fee,
  Ne none rich weed;
There is a child in Bethlehem born
  Shall helpen us at our need."

"That is all so sooth, Stephen,
 Asll so sooth, I-wis,
As this capon crowè shall
 That lieth here in my dish."

That word was not so soon said,
 That word in that hall,
The capon crew *Christus natus est*
 Among the lordès all.

"Riseth up, my tormentors,
 By two and all by one,
And leadeth Stephen out of this town,
 And stoneth him with stone."

Tooken they Stephen
 And stoned him in the way,
And therefore in his even
 On Christès own day.

The Oxen

THOMAS HARDY

Christmas Eve, and twelve of the clock.
　　"Now they are all on their knees,"
An elder said as we sat in a flock
　　By the embers in hearthside ease.

We pictured the meek milk creatures where
　　They dwelt in their strawy pen,
Nor did it occur to one of us there
　　To doubt they were kneeling then.

So fair a fancy few would weave
　　In these years! Yet, I feel,
If someone said on Christmas eve,
　　"Come; see the oxen kneel,

"In the lonely barton by yonder coomb
　　Our childhood used to know,"
I should go with him in the gloom,
　　Hoping it might be so.

It Came Upon the Midnight Clear

EDMUND HAMILTON SEARS

It came upon the midnight clear,
    That glorious song of old,
From angels bending near the earth
    To touch their harps of gold:
"Peace on earth, good will to men,
    From heav'n's all-gracious King."
The world in solemn stillness lay
    To hear the angels sing.

Still through the cloven skies they come
    With peaceful wings unfurled,
And still their heav'nly music floats
    O'er all the weary world;
Above its sad and lowly plains
    They bend on hov'ring wing,
And ever o'er its Babel-sounds
    The blessed angels sing.

Yet with the woes of sin an strife
    The world has suffered long;
Beneath the heav'nly strain have rolled
    Two thousand years of wrong;
And man, at war with man, hears not
    The tidings which they bring;
O hush the noise, ye men of strife,
    And hear the angels sing!

O ye, beneath life's crushing load,
    Whose forms are bending low,
Who toil along the climbing way
    With painful steps and slow,
Look now! for glad and golden hours
    Come swiftly on the wing;
O rest beside the weary road
    And hear the angels sing!

For lo! the days are hast'ning on,
    By prophets seen of old,
When with the ever-circling years
    Shall come the time foretold,
When peace shall over all the earth
    Its ancient splendors fling,
And the whole world give back the song
    Which now the angels sing.

THE BLESSED
JOURNEY

The Cherry Tree Carol

TRADITIONAL ENGLISH CAROL

When Joseph was an old man,
An old man was he,
He married Virgin Mary,
The Queen of Galilee
He married Virgin Mary
The Queen of Galilee

Then Mary spoke to Joseph,
So meek and so mild,
"Joseph, gather me some cherries,
For I am with child.
Joseph, gather me some cherries,
For I am with child."

Then Joseph grew in anger,
In anger grew he:
"Let the father of thy baby
Gather cherries for thee."

Then Jesus spoke a few words,
A few words spoke He:
"Let my mother have some cherries,
Bow low down, cherry tree!
Let my mother have some cherries,
Bow low down, cherry tree!"

The cherry tree bowed down,
Bowed low down to the ground,
And Mary gathered cherries
While Joseph stood around,
And Mary gathered cherries
While Joseph stood around.

Then Joseph took Mary
All on his right knee.
"What have I done, oh, Lord,
Have mercy on me,
What have I done, oh, Lord,
Have mercy on me."

As Joseph Was A-Walking

AUTHOR UNKNOWN

As Joseph was a-walking
    He heard Angels sing,
"This night shall be born
    Our Heavenly King.

"He neither shall be born
    In house nor in hall.
Nor in the place of paradise,
    But in an ox-stall.

"He neither shall be clothèd
    In purple nor in pall;
But all in fair linen,
    As wear babies all.

"He neither shall be rockèd
    In silver nor gold,

But in a wooden cradle
    That rocks on the mould.

"He neither shall be christened
    In milk nor in wine,
But in pure spring-well water
    Fresh spring from Bethine."

Mary took her baby,
    She dressed Him so sweet,
She laid Him in a manger,
    All there for to sleep.

As she stood over Him
    She heard Angels sing,
"Oh, bless our dear Saviour
    Our Heavenly King!"

Coventry Carol

ROBERT CROO

Lully, lullay, Thou little tiny Child,
By, by, lully, lullay:
Lullay, Thou little tiny child,
By, by, lully, lullay.

O sisters too, how may we do
For to preserve this day,
This poor Youngling for whom we do sing,
By, by, lully, lullay?

Herod the king in his raging,
Charged he hath this day,
His men of might, in his own sight,
All children young to slay.

Then woe is me, poor Child, for Thee,
And ever mourn and say,
For Thy parting nor say, nor sing,
By, by, lully, lullay.

The House of Christmas

G.K. CHESTERTON

There fared a mother driven forth
    Out of an inn to roam;
In the place where she was homeless
    All men are at home.
The crazy stable close at hand,
With shaking timber and shifting sand,
Grew a stronger thing to abide and stand
    Than the square stones of Rome.

For men are homesick in their homes,
    And strangers under the sun,
And they lay their heads in a foreign land
    Whenever the day is done.
Here we have battle and blazing eyes,
And chance and honour and high surprise;
But our homes are under miraculous skies
    Where the Yule tale was begun.

A child in a foul stable,
    Where the beats feed and foam;
Only where He was homeless
    Are you and I at home;
We have hands that fashion and heads that know,
But our hearts we lost—how long ago!—
In a place no chart nor ship can show
    Under the sky's dome.

    And strangle the plain things are,
The earth is enough and the air is enough
    For our wonder and our war;
But our rest is as far as the fire-drake swings,
And our peace is put in impossible things
Where clashed and thundered unthinkable wings
    Round an incredible star.

To an open house in the evening
    Home shall men come,
To an older place than Eden
    And a taller town than Rome;
To the end of the way of the wandering star,
To the things that cannot be and that are,
To the place where Go was homeless
    And all men are at home.

How Far Is It to Bethlehem

FRANCES CHESTERTON

How far is it to Bethlehem?
  Not very far.
Shall we find the stable-room
  Lit by a star?

Can we see the little Child,
  Is He within?
If we lift the wooden latch
  May we go in?

May we stroke the creatures there,
  Ox, ass, or sheep?
May we peep like them and see
  Jesus asleep?

If we touch His tiny hand
  Will He awake?

Will He know we've come so far
    Just for his sake?

Great Kings have precious gifts,
    And we have naught;
Little smiles and little tears
    Are all we brought.

For all weary children
    Mary must weep.
Here, on His bed of straw,
    Sleep, children, sleep.

God, in his Mother's arms
    Babes in the byre,
Sleep, as they sleep who find
    Their heart's desire.

The Barn

ELIZABETH COATSWORTH

"I am tired of this barn!" said the colt.
"And every day it snows.
Outside there's no grass any more
And icicles grow on my nose.
I am tired of hearing the cows
Breathing and talking together.
I am sick of these clucking hens.
I *hate* stables and winter weather!"

"Hush, little colt," said the mare
"And a story I will tell
Of a barn like this one of ours
And the wonders that there befell.
It was weather much like this,
And the beasts stood as we stand now
In the warm good dark of the barn—
A horse and an ass and a cow."

"And sheep?" asked the colt. "Yes, sheep,
And a pig and a goat and a hen
All of the beasts of the barnyard,
The usual servants of men.
And into their midst came a lady
And she was cold as death,
But the animals leaned abover her
and made her warm with their breath.

"There was her baby born
And laid to sleep in the hay,
While music flooded the rafters
And the bard was as light as day.
And angels and kings and shepherds
Came to worship the babe from afar,
But we looked at him first of all the creatures
By the bright strange light of a star!"

The Stable

GABRIELA MISTRAL

When midnight came
and the Child's first cry arose,
a hundred beasts awaked
and the stable became alive.

And dawing near they came
reaching out toward the Child
a hundred eager necks
like a forest swaying.

And ox whose eyes were as tender
as though filled with dew,
lowered its head to breathe
quietly in His face.

Against Him rubbed a lamb
with the softest of fleece,
and two baby goats squatted,
licking His hands.

The walls of the stable
unnoticed were covered
with pheasants and with geese
and cocks and with blackbirds.

The pheasants flew down
and swept over the Child
tails of many colors;
while the geese with wide bills
soothed His pallet of straw;
and a swarm of blackbirds
became a veil rising and falling
above the new born.

The Virgin, confused among such horns
and whiteness of breathing,
fluttered hither and yon
unable to pick up her Child.

And Joseph arrived laughing
to help her in her confusion,
and the upset stable was like
a forest in the wind.

O Little Town of Bethlehem

PHILLIPS BROOKS

O little town of Bethlehem!
How still we see thee lie;
Above thy deep and dreamless sleep
The silent stars go by;
Yet in thy dark streets shineth
The everlasting Light;
The hopes and fears of all the years
Are met in thee tonight.

For Christ is born of Mary,
And gathered all above,
While mortals sleep, the angels keep
Their watch of wondering love.
O morning stars, together
Proclaim, the holy birth!
And praises sing to God the King,
And peace to men on earth.

How silently, how silently,
The wondrous gift is giv'n!
So God imparts to human hearts
The blessings of His heav'n.
No ear may hear His coming,
But in this world of sin,
Where meek souls will receive Him still,
The dear Christ enters in.

O holy Child of Bethlehem!
Descend to us, we pray;
Cast out our sin and enter in,
Be born in us today.
We hear the Christmas angels
The great glad tidings tell;
O come to us, abide with us,
Our Lord Emmanuel!

A Christmas Folk-Song

LISETTE WOODWORTH REESE

The little Jesus came to town;
The wind blew up, the wind blew down;
Out in the street the wind was bold;
Now who would house Him from the cold?

Then opened wide a stable door,
Fair were the rushes on the floor;
The Ox put forth a hornèd head:
"Come, little Lord, here make Thy bed."

Uprose the Sheep were folded near:
"Thou Lamb of God, come, enter here."
He entered there to rush the reed,
Who was the Lamb of God indeed.

The little Jesus came to town;
With ox and sheep He laid Him down;
Peace to the byre, peace to the fold,
For that they housed Him from the cold!

Christmas Carol

MAY PROBYN

Lacking samite and sable,
  Lacking silver and gold,
The Prince Jesus in the poor stable
  Slept, and was three hours old.

As doves by the fair water,
  Mary, not touched of sin,
Sat by Him—the King's daughter,
  All glorious within.

A lily without one stain, a
  Star where no spot hath room.
Ave, gratia plena—
  Virgo Virginum!

Clad not in pearl-sewn vesture,
  Clad not in cramoisie,
She hath hushed, she hath cradled to rest, her
  God the first time on her knee.

Where is one to adore Him?
  The ox hath dumbly confessed,
With the ass, meek kneeling before Him,
  Et homo factus est.

Not throned on ivory or cedar,
  Not crowned with a Queen's crown,
At her breast it is Mary shall feed her
  Maker, from Heaven come down.

The trees in Paradise blossom
  Sudden, and its bells chime—
She giveth Him, held to her bosom,
  Her immaculate milk the first time.

The night with wings of angels
  Was alight, and its snow-packed ways
Sweet made (say the Evangels)
  With the noise of their virelays.

Quem vidistis, pastores?
  Why go ye feet unshod?
Wot ye within yon door is
  Mary, the Mother of God?

No smoke of spice is ascending
  There—no roses are piled—

But, choicer than all balms blending,
  There Mary hath kissed her child.

Dilectus meus mihi
  Et ego illi—cold
Small cheek against her cheek, He
  Sleepeth, three hours old.

The Seven Joys of Mary

TRADITIONAL ENGLISH CAROL

The first good joy that Mary had,
It was the joy of one;
To see the blessed Jesus Christ
When he was first her son
When he was first her son

Good man and blessed may he be,
Both Father, Son, and Holy Ghost,
To all eternity.

The next good joy that Mary had,
It was the joy of two,
To see her own Son, Jesus Christ,
To make the lame to go.
To make the lame to go.

Good man and blessed may he be,
Both Father, Son, and Holy Ghost,
To all eternity.

The next good joy that Mary had,
It was the joy of three;
To see her own son, Jesus Christ,
To make the blind to see:
To make the blind to see:

Good man and blessed may he be,
Both Father, Son, and Holy Ghost,
To all eternity.

The next good joy that Mary had,
It was the joy of four;
To see her own son, Jesus Christ,
To read the bible o'er:
To read the bible o'er:

Good man and blessed may he be,
Both Father, Son, and Holy Ghost,
To all eternity.

The next good joy that Mary had,
It was the joy of five;
To see her own son, Jesus Christ,
To bring the dead alive:
To bring the dead alive:

Good man and blessed may he be,
Both Father, Son, and Holy Ghost,
To all eternity.

The next good joy that Mary had,
It was the joy of six;
To see her own son, Jesus Christ,
Upon the crucifix:
Upon the crucifix:

Good man and blessed may he be,
Both Father, Son, and Holy Ghost,
To all eternity.

The next good joy that Mary had,
It was the joy of seven;
To see her own son, Jesus Christ,
To wear the crown of heaven:
To wear the crown of heaven:

Good man and blessed may he be,
Both Father, Son, and Holy Ghost,
To all eternity.

The Peaceful Night

JOHN MILTON

But peaceful was the night
Wherein the Prince of Light
    His reign of peace upon the earth began.
The winds with wonder whist,
Smoothly the waters kist,
    Whispering new joys to the mild Ocean,—
Who now hath quite forgot to rave,
While birds of calm sit brooding on the charmèd wave.

The stars, with deep amaze,
Stand fixed in steadfast gaze,
    Bending one way their precious influence;
And will not take their flight,
For all the morning light,
    Or Lucifer that often warned them thence;
But in their glimmering orbs did glow,
Until their Lord himself bespake, and bid them go.

And, though the shady gloom
Had given day her room,
  The sun himself withheld his wonted speed,
And hid his head for shame,
As his inferior flame
  The new-enlightened world no more should need:
He saw a greater Sun appear
Than his bright throne or burning axeltree could bear.

A Christmas Carol

G. K. CHESTERTON

The Christ-child lay on Mary's lap,
    His hair was like a light.
(O weary, weary were the world,
    But here is all aright.)

The Christ-child lay on Mary's breast,
    His hair was like a star.
(O stern and cunning are the kings,
    But here the true hearts are.)

The Christ-child lay on Mary's heart,
    His hair was like a fire.
(O weary, weary is the world,
    But here the world's desire.)

The Christ-child stood at Mary's knee,
    His hair was like a crown,
And all the flowers looked up at Him,
    And all the stars looked down.

Christmas Carol

SARA TEASDALE

The kings they came from out the south,
All dressed in ermine fine;
They bore Him gold and chrysoprase,
And gifts of precious wine.

The shepherds came from out the north,
Their coats were brown and old;
They brought Him little new-born lambs—
They had not any gold.

The wise men came from out the east,
And they were wrapped in white;
The start that led them all the way
Did glorify the night.

The angels came from heaven high,
And they were clad with wings;
And lo, they brought a joyful song
The host of heaven sings.

The kings they knocked upon the door,
　　The wise men entered in,
The shepherds followed after them
　　To hear the song begin.

The angels sang through all the night.
　　Until the rising sun,
But little Jesus fell asleep
　　Before the song was done.

THE
GUIDING
STAR

As I Sat Under a Sycamore Tree

AUTHOR UNKNOWN

As I sat under a sycamore tree,
A sycamore tree, a sycamore tree,
I looked me out upon the sea
On Christ's Sunday at morn.

I saw three ships a-sailing there,
A-sailing there, a-sailing there,
Jesus, Mary and Joseph they bare
On Christ's Sunday at morn.

Joseph did whistle and Mary did sing,
Mary did sing, Mary did sing,
And all the bells on earth did ring
For joy our Lord was born.

O they sail'd in to Bethlehem!
To Bethlehem, to Bethlehem;

Saint Michael was the sterèsman,
Saint John sate in the horn.

And all the bells on earth did ring
    On earth did ring, on earth did ring:
Welcome be thou Heaven's King,
On Christ's Sunday at morn!

I Saw Three Ships

AUTHOR UNKNOWN

I saw three ships come sailing in,
    On Christmas day, on Christmas day,
I saw three ships come sailing in,
    On Christmas day, in the morning.

And what was in those ships all three
    On Christmas day, on Christmas day...
And what was in those ships all three
    On Christmas day, in the morning.

The Virgin Mary and Christ were there,
    On Christmas day, on Christmas day,
Our Savior Christ and his lady,
    On Christmas day, in the morning.

Pray, whither sailed those ships all three,
    On Christmas day, on Christmas day?
Pray, whither sailed those ships all three
    On Christmas day, in the morning.

Oh, they sailed into Bethlehem,
    On Christmas day, on Christmas day;
Oh, they sailed into Bethlehem,
    On Christmas day, in the morning.

And all the bells on earth shall ring,
    On Christmas day, on Christmas day;
And all the bells on earth shall ring,
    On Christmas day, in the morning.

And all the angels in heaven shall sing,
    On Christmas day, on Christmas day;
And all the angels in heaven shall sing,
    On Christmas day, in the morning.

And all the souls on earth shall sing
    On Christmas day, on Christmas day;
And all the souls on earth shall sing
    On Christmas day, in the morning.

Then let us all rejoice amain!
    On Christmas day, on Christmas day...
Then let us all rejoice amain!
    On Christmas day, in the morning.

The Three Ships

As I went up the mountain-side
The sea below me glitter'd wide,
And, Eastward, far away, I spied
    On Christmas Day, on Christmas Day,
The three great ships that take the tide
    On Christmas Day in the morning.

Ye have heard the song, how these must ply
From the harbours of home to the ports o' the sky!
Do ye dream none knowth the whither and why
    On Christmas Day, on Christmas Day
The three great ships go sailing by
    On Christmas Day in the morning?

Yet, as I live, I never knew
That ever a song could ring so true,
Till I saw them break thro' a haze of blue
    On Christmas Day, on Christmas Day;

And the marvellous ancient flags they flew
　　On Christmas Day in the morning!

From the heights above the belfried town
I saw that the sails were patched and brown,
But the flags were a-flame with a great renown
　　On Christmas Day, on Christmas Day,
And on every mast was a golden crown
　　On Christmas Day in the morning.

Most marvellous ancient ships were these!
Were their prows a-plunge to the Chersonese,
For the pomp of Rome, or the glory of Greece,
　　On Christmas Day, on Christmas Day?
Were they out on a quest for the Golden Fleece
　　On Christmas Day in the morning?

The sun and the wind they told me there
How goodly a load the three ships bear,
For the first is gold and the second is myrrh
　　On Christmas Day, on Christmas Day;
And the third is frankincense most rare,
　　On Christmas Day in the morning.

They have mixed their shrouds with the golden sky,
They have faded away where the last dreams die...

Ah yet, will ye watch, when the mist lifts high
    On Christmas Day, on Christmas Day?
Will ye see three ships come sailing by
    On Christmas Day in the morning?

Carol of the Brown King

LANGSTON HUGHES

Of the three Wise Men
Who came to the King,
One was a brown man,
So they sing.

Of the three Wise Men
Who followed the Star,
One was a brown king
From afar.

They brought fine gifts
Of spices and gold
In jeweled boxes
Of beauty untold.

Unto His humble
Manger they came
And bowed their heads
In Jesus' name.
Three Wise Men,
One dark like me –
Part of His
Nativity.

The Kings of the East

KATHERINE LEE BATES

The Kings of the East are riding
    To-night to Bethlehem.
The sunset glows dividing,
The Kings of the East are riding;
A star their journey guiding,
    Gleaming with gold and gem
The Kings of the East are riding
    To-night to Bethlehem.

To a strange sweet harp of Zion
    The starry host troops forth;
The golden glaived Orion
To a strange sweet harp of Zion;
The Archer and the Lion,
    The watcher of the North;
To a strange sweet harp of Zion
    The starry host troops forth.

There beams above a manger
    The child-face of a star;
Amid the stars a stranger,
It beams above a manger;
What means this ether-ranger
    To pause where poor folk are?
There beams above a manger
    The child-face of a star.

Three Kings of Orient

A Christmas Carol

We three kings of Orient are,
Bearing gifts we traverse afar,
    Field and Fountain,
    Moor and Mountain,
Following yonder star.

O Star of wonder, Star of Night,
Star with royal beauty bright,
    Westward leading,
    Still proceeding,
Guide us to Thy perfect light.

Born a king on Bethlehem plain,
Gold I bring to crown Him again,
    King for ever,
    Ceasing never
Over us all to reign.

O Star of wonder, Star of Night,
Star with royal beauty bright,
Westward leading,
Still proceeding,
Guide us to Thy perfect light.

Frankincense to offer have I,
Incense owns a Diety nigh:
Prayer and praising
All men raising,
Worship Him God on High.

O Star of wonder, Star of Night,
Star with royal beauty bright,
Westward leading,
Still proceeding,
Guide us to Thy perfect light.

Myrrh is mine; its bitter perfume
Breathes a life of gathering gloom;
Sorrowing, sighing,
Bleeding, dying,
Sealed in the stone-cold tomb.

Glorious now behold Him arise,
King, and God, and Sacrifice;
Heav'n sings

Alleluia, Alleluia
The earth replies.

O Star of wonder, Star of Night,
Star with royal beauty bright,
    Westward leading,
    Still proceeding,
Guide us to Thy perfect light.

Ballad of the Epiphany

CHARLES DALMON

When Christ was born in Bethlehem,
    Pan left his Sussex Downs,
To see three kings go riding by,
    All in their robes and crowns;
And, as they went in royal state,
    Pan followed them, unseen,
Though tiny tufts of grass and flowers
    Showed where his feet had been.

And when to Bethlehem they came,
    Birds sang in every tree,
And Mary in the stable sat,
    With Jesus on her knee;
And while the oxen munched their hay,
    The kings with one accord
Placed gold and frankincense and myrrh
    Before their infant Lord.

And when Pan peeped upon the scene,
 The Christ-Child clapped His hands,
And chuckled with delight to see
 The god of pasture lands;
And Mary sang *"Magnificat"*
 Above the kneeling kings,
And angels circled overhead
 On rainbow-colored wings.

And many a little singing bird
 Flew past the open door
To hop and chirrup in the straw
 Above the stable floor;
Wrens, robins, linnets, greenfinches,
 And many another one,
Flew in to show good fellowship
 With Mary's newborn Son.

Then Pan stood up and played his pipes
 Beside the manger-bed,
And every little bird went near
 And raised its faithful head;
And one, most beautiful to see,
 A fair and milk-white dove,
Arose and hovered in the air
 To testify its love.

But when the kings looked up to find
    Who made the piping sound,
They only saw white lilies shine,
    Fresh-gathered, on the ground,
And through the doorway, and beyond,
    A shaggy wild goat leap;
And, in its gentle mother's arm,
    The Baby fast asleep.

The Three Kings

HENRY WADSWORTH LONGFELLOW

Three Kings came riding from far away,
    Melchoir and Gaspar and Baltasar;
Three Wise Men out of the East were they,
And they traveled by night and they slept by day,
    For their guide was a beautiful, wonderful star.

The star was so beautiful, large and clear,
    That all the other stars of the sky
Became a white mist in the atmosphere;
And by this they knew that the coming was near
    Of the Prince foretold in the prophecy.

Three caskets they bore on their saddle-bows,
    Three caskets of gold with golden keys;
Their robes were of crimson silk, with rows
Of bells and pomegranates and furbelows,
    Their turbans like blossoming almond-trees.

And so the Three Kings rode into the West,
  Through the dusk of night over hill and dell,
And sometimes they nodded with beard on breast,
And sometimes talked, and they paused to rest,
  With the people they met at some wayside well.

"Of the Child that is born," said Baltasar,
  "Good people, I pray you, tell us the news;
For we in the East have seen His star,
And have ridden fast, and have ridden far,
  To find and worship the King of the Jews."

And the people answered, "You ask in vain;
  We know of no king but Herod the Great!"
They thought the Wise Men were men insane,
As they spurred their horses across the plain
  Like riders in haste who cannot wait.

And when they came to Jerusalem,
  Herod the Great, who had heard this thing,
Sent for the Wise Men and questioned them;
And said, "Go down unto Bethlehem,
  And bring me tidings of this new king."

So they rode away, and the star stood still,
  The only one in the gray of morn;
Yes, it stopped, it stood still of its own free will,

Right over Bethlehem on the hill,
    The city of David where Christ was born.

And the Three Kings rode through the gate and the guard,
    Through the silent street, till their horses turned
And neighed as they entered the great inn-yard;
But the windows were closed, and the doors were barred,
    And only a light in the stable burned.

And cradled there in the scented hay,
    In the air made sweet by the breath on kine,
The little Child in the manger lay,
The Child that would be King one day
    Of a kingdom not human, but divine.

His mother, Mary of Nazareth,
    Sat watching beside his place of rest,
Watching the even flow of his breath,
For the joy of life and the terror of death
    Were mingled together in her breast.

They laid their offerings at his feet:
    The gold was their tribute to a King;
The frankincense, with its odor sweet,
Was for the Priest, the Paraclete;
    The myrrh for the body's burying.

And the mother wondered and bowed her head,
    And sat as still as a statue of stone;
Her heart was troubled yet comforted,
Remembering what the angel had said
    Of an endless reign and of David's throne.

Then the Kings rode out of the city gate,
    With a clatter of hoofs in proud array;
But they went not back to Herod the Great,
For they knew his malice and feared his hate,
    And returned to their homes by another way.

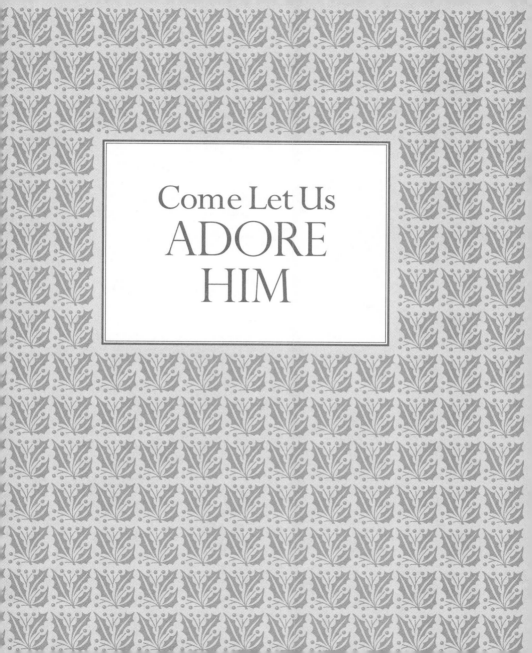

Come Let Us
ADORE
HIM

Before the Paling of the Stars

CHRISTINA ROSSETTI

Before the paling of the stars,
    Before the winter morn,
Before the earliest cockcrow,
    Jesus Christ was born:
Born in a stable,
    Cradled in a manger,
In the world His hands had made
    Born a stranger.

Priest and king lay fast asleep
    In Jerusalem,
Young and old lay fast asleep
    In crowded Bethlehem;
Saint and Angel, ox and ass,
    Kept a watch together
Before the Christmas daybreak
    In the winter weather.

Jesus on his mother's breast
In the stable cold,
Spotless Lamb of God was He,
Shepherd of the fold:
Let us kneel with Mary maid,
With Joseph bent and hoary,
With Saint and Angel, ox and ass,
To hail the King of Glory.

Christus Natus Est

COUNTEE CULLEN

In Bethlehem
On Christmas morn,
The lowly gem
Of love was born.
Hosannah! *Christus natus est.*

Bright in her crown
Of fiery star,
Judea's town
Shown from afar:
Hosannah! *Christus natus est.*

While beasts in stall,
On bended knee,
Did carol all
Most joyously:
Hosannah! *Christus natus est.*

For bird and beast
He did not come,

But for the least
Of mortal scum.
Hosannah! *Christus natus est.*

Who lies in ditch?
Who begs his bread?
Who has no stitch
For back or head?
Hosannah! *Christus natus est.*

Who wakes to weep,
Lies down to mourn?
Who in his sleep
Withdraws from scorn?
Hosannah! *Christus natus est.*

Ye outraged dust,
On field and plain,
To feed the lust
Of madmen slain:
Hosannah! *Christus natus est.*

The manger still
Outshines the throne;
Christ must and will
Come to his own.
Hosannah! *Christus natus est.*

A Christmas Hymn

RICHARD WATSON GILDER

Tell me what is this innumerable throng
Singing in the heavens a loud angelic song?
These are they who come with swift and shining feet
From round about the throne of God the Lord of Light to greet.

O, who are these that hasten beneath the starry sky,
As if with joyful tidings that through the world shall fly?
The faithful shepherds these, who greatly were afeared
When, as they watched their flocks by night, the heavenly host appeared.

Who are these that follow across the hills of night
A star that westward hurries along the fields of light?
Three wise men from the east who myrrh and treasure bring
To lay them at the feet of him, their Lord and Christ and King.

What babe new-born is this that in a manger cries?
Near on her bed of pain his happy mother lies.
O, see! the air is shaken with white and heavenly wings—

This is the Lord of all the earth, this is the King of kings.
Tell me, how may I join in this holy feast
With all the kneeling world, and I of all the least?
Fear not, O faithful heart, but bring what most is meet;
Bring love alone, true love alone, and lay it at his feet.

A Hymn for Christmas Day

THOMAS CHATTERTON

Almighty Framer of the skies!
Oh, let our pure devotion rise
　　Like incense in Thy sight!
Wrapt in impenetrable shade,
The texture of our souls were made,
　　Til Thy command gave light.

The Sun of Glory gleam'd the ray,
Refined the darkness into day,
　　And bid the vapours fly:
Impell'd by His eternal Love,
He left His palaces above
　　To cheer our gloomy sky.

How shall we celebrate the day
When God appear'd in mortal clay,
　　The mark of worldly scorn:

When the archangel's heavenly lays
Attempted the Redeemer's praise,
   And hail'd salvation's morn!

A humble form of Godhead wore,
The pains of poverty He bore,
   To gaudy pomp unknown:
Though in a human walk He trod,
Still was the Man Almighty God,
   In glory all His own.

Despis'd, oppress'd, the Godhead bears
The torments of this vale of tears,
   Nor bade His vengeance rise;
He saw the creatures He had made
Revile his power, his peace invade—
   He saw with Mercy's eyes.

How shall we celebrate His name,
Who groaned beneath a life of shame,
   In all afflictions tried!
The soul is raptur'd to conceive
A truth which Being must believe—
   The God eternal died.

My soul, exert thy powers—adore;
Upon Devotion's plumage soar
   To celebrate the day;
The God from whom creation sprung
Shall animate my grateful tongue;
   From Him I'll catch the lay!

Hark! The Herald Angels Sing

CHARLES WESLEY

Hark! the herald angels sing
"Glory to the newborn King!
Peace on earth and mercy mild
God and sinners reconciled!"
Joyful, all ye nations rise
Join the triumph of the skies
With the angelic host proclaim:
"Christ is born in Bethlehem!"
Hark! the herald angels sing
"Glory to the newborn King!"

Christ by highest heav'n adored
Christ the everlasting Lord!
Late in time behold Him come
Offspring of a Virgin's womb.
Veiled in flesh the Godhead see;
Hail the incarnate Deity,

Pleased as man with man to dwell,
Jesus, our Emmanuel
Hark! the herald angels sing
"Glory to the newborn King!"

Hail the heav'n-born Prince of Peace!
Hail the Son of Righteousness!
Light and life to all He brings,
Ris'n with healing in His wings.
Mild He lays His glory by,
Born that man no more may die,
Born to raise the songs of earth,
Born to give them second birth.
Hark! The herald angels sing
"Glory to the newborn King!"

Whence Comes This Rush of Wings?

TRADITIONAL FRENCH CAROL

Whence comes this rush of wings afar,
Following straight the Noël star?
Birds from the woods in wondrous flight,
Bethlehem seek this Holy Night.

"Tell us, ye birds, why come ye here,
Into this stable, poor and drear?"
"Hast'ning we seek the new-born King,
And all our sweetest music bring."

Hark! how the greenfinch bears his part,
Philomel, too, with tender heart,
Chants from her leafy dark retreat,
Re, mi, fa, sol, in accents sweet.

Angels and shepherds, birds of the sky,
Come where the Son of God doth lie;
Christ on earth with man doth dwell,
Join the shout, "Noël, Noël!"

O Come, All Ye Faithful

LATIN CAROL

Translated by Frederick Oakeley

O come, all ye faithful,
Joyful and triumphant;
O come ye, O come ye to Bethlehem;
Come and behold Him
Born the king of angels;

O come, let us adore Him,
O come, let us adore Him,
O come, let us adore Him,
Christ the Lord.

Sing, choirs of angels,
Sing in exultation,
Sing all ye citizens of heav'n above:
Glory to god, all glory
In the highest.

O come, let us adore Him,
O come, let us adore Him,
O come, let us adore Him,
Christ the Lord.

See how the shepherds,
Summoned to his cradle,
Leaving their flocks, draw nigh to gaze;
We too will thither
Bend our joyful footsteps;

O come, let us adore Him,
O come, let us adore Him,
O come, let us adore Him,
Christ the Lord.

Child, for us sinners,
Poor and in the manger,
We would embrace thee, with love and awe;
Who would not love thee,
Loving us so dearly?

O come, let us adore Him,
O come, let us adore Him,
O come, let us adore Him,
Christ the Lord.

Yea, Lord, we greet Thee,
Born this happy morning;
Jesus to Thee be glory giv'n;
Word of the Father,
Now in flesh appearing.

O come, let us adore Him,
O come, let us adore Him,
O come, let us adore Him,
Christ the Lord.

A Child This Day Is Born

TRADITIONAL ENGLISH CAROL

A child this day is born,
A child of high renown,
Most worth of a sceptre,
A sceptre and a crown:

> Nowell, Nowell, Nowell,
> Nowell, sing all we may,
> Because the King of all kings
> Was born this blessèd day.

These tidings shepherds heard,
In field watching their fold,
Were by an angel unto them
That night revealed and told:

> Nowell, Nowell, Nowell,
> Nowell, sing all we may,

Because the King of all kings
Was born this blessèd day.

To whom the angel spoke,
Saying, "Be not afraid;
Be glad, poor silly shepherds—
Why are you so dismayed?

Nowell, Nowell, Nowell,
Nowell, sing all we may,
Because the King of all kings
Was born this blessèd day.

"For lo! I bring you tidings
Of gladness and of mirth,
Which cometh to all people by
This holy infant's birth":

Nowell, Nowell, Nowell,
Nowell, sing all we may,
Because the King of all kings
Was born this blessèd day.

Then there was with the angel
A host incontinent
Of heavenly bright soldiers,
Which from the Highest was sent:

Nowell, Nowell, Nowell,
Nowell, sing all we may,
Because the King of all kings
Was born this blessèd day.

Lauding the Lord our God,
And His celestial King;
All glory be in Paradise,
This heavenly host did sing:

Nowell, Nowell, Nowell,
Nowell, sing all we may,
Because the King of all kings
Was born this blessèd day.

And as the angels told them
So to them did appear;
They found the young child, Jesus Christ,
With Mary, His mother dear.

Nowell, Nowell, Nowell,
Nowell, sing all we may,
Because the King of all kings
Was born this blessèd day.

While Shepherds Watched Their Flocks By Night

NAHUM TATE

While shepherds wacth'd their flocks by night,
All seated on the ground,
The angel of the Lord came down,
And glory shone around
       And glory shone around

"Fear not!" said he, for mighty dread
Had seized their troubled mind,
"Glad tidings of great joy I bring,
To you and all mankind.
       To you and all mankind.

"To you, in David's town, this day
Is born of David's line
The Savior who is Christ the Lord,
And this shall be the sign,
       And this shall be the sign.

"The Heav'nly Babe you there shall find
To human view displayed,
All meanly wrapped in swathing band
And in a manger laid,
    And in a manger laid.

Thus spake the seraph and forthwith
Appeared a shining throng
Of angels, praising God, who thus
Addressed their joyful song,
    Addressed their joyful song:

"All glory be to God on high,
And to the earth be peace;
Goodwill henceforth from heav'n to men
Begin, and never cease,
    Begin, and never cease!"

What Child Is This?

WILLIAM CHATTERTON DIX

What Child is this, who, laid to rest
On Mary's lap, is sleeping?
Whom angels greet with anthems sweet,
While shepherds watch are keeping?

This, this is Christ the King,
Whom shepherds guard and angels sing;
Haste, haste to bring Him laud,
The Babe, the Son of Mary.

Why lies He in such mean estate,
Where ox and ass are feeding?
Good Christians fear: for sinners here
The silent Word is pleading.

This, this is Christ the King,
Whom shepherds guard and angels sing;
Haste, haste to bring Him laud,
The Babe, the Son of Mary.

So bring Him incense, gold, and myrrh,
Come peasant, King to own Him;
The King of Kings salvation brings;
Let loving hearts enthrone Him!

This, this is Christ the King,
Whom shepherds guard and angels sing;
Haste, haste to bring Him laud,
The Babe, the Son of Mary.

Raise, raise the song on high,
The Virgin sings her lullaby:
Joy, joy for Christ is born,
The Babe, the son of Mary!

Angels We Have Heard on High

TRADITIONAL FRENCH CAROL

Angels we have heard on high,
sweetly singing o'er the plains;
And the mountains in reply
Echoing their joyous strains

Gloria in excelsis Deo,
Gloria in excelsis Deo.

Shepherds, why this jubilee?
Why your joyous strains prolong?
What the gladsome tidings be
Which inspire your heav'nly song?

Gloria in excelsis Deo,
Gloria in excelsis Deo.

Come to Bethlehem, and see
Him whose birth the angels sing;

Come, adore on bended knee,
Christ, the Lord, the new-born King.

Gloria in excelsis Deo,
Gloria in excelsis Deo.

See Him in a manger laid,
Whom the choir of angels praise;
Holy Spirit, lend thine aid,
While out hearts in love we raise.

Gloria in excelsis Deo,
Gloria in excelsis Deo.

The Holy Night

ELIZABETH BARRETT BROWNING

We sate among the stalls at Bethlehem;
The dumb kine from their fodder turning them,
    Softened their hornèd faces
    To almost human gazes
    Toward the newly Born:
The simple shepherds from the star-lit brooks
    Brought visionary looks,
As yet in their astonied hearing rung
    The strange sweet angel-tongue:
The magi of the East, in sandals worn,
    Knelt reverent, sweeping round,
    With long pale beards, their gifts upon
        the ground,
    The incense, myrrh, and gold
These baby hands were impotent to hold:
So let all earthlies and celestials wait
    Upon thy royal state.
    Sleep, sleep, my kingly One!

The First Nowell

TRADITIONAL ENGLISH CAROL

The first Nowell the Angel did say,
Was to certain poor shepherds in fields as they lay;
In fields where they lay keeping their sheep,
On a cold winter's night that was so deep.

Nowell, Nowell, Nowell, Nowell,
Born is the King of Israel.

The looked up and saw a star
Shining in the east, beyond them far;
And to the earth it gave great light,
And so it continued, both day and night.

Nowell, Nowell, Nowell, Nowell,
Born is the King of Israel.

And by the light of the same star,
Three wise men came from country far;
To seek for a king was their intent,
And to follow the star wherever it went.

Nowell, Nowell, Nowell, Nowell,
Born is the King of Israel.

The star drew nigh to the northwest,
O'er Bethlehem it took its rest,
And there it did both stop and stay
Right over the place where Jesus lay.

Nowell, Nowell, Nowell, Nowell,
Born is the King of Israel.

Then entered in those wisemen three,
Full reverently upon the knee,
And offered there, in His presence,
Their gold and myrrh and frankincense.

Nowell, Nowell, Nowell, Nowell,
Born is the King of Israel.

Then let us all with one accord
Sing praises to our heav'nly Lord;
That hath made heaven and earth of naught,
And with his blood mankind hath bought.

Nowell, Nowell, Nowell, Nowell,
Born is the King of Israel.

Away In a Manger

AUTHOR UNKNOWN

Away in a manger,
No crib for his bed,
The little Lord Jesus
Laid down his sweet head.
The stars in the sky
Look'd down where he lay,
The little Lord Jesus
Asleep on the hay.

The cattle are lowing,
The baby awakes,
But little Lord Jesus
No crying he makes.
I love thee, Lord Jesus!
Look down from the sky,
And stay by my cradle
Till morning is nigh.

Be near me, Lord Jesus;
I ask thee to stay
Close by me forever,
And love me, I pray.
Bless all the dear children
In thy tender care,
And fit us for heaven,
To live with thee there.

Angels from
the Realms of Glory

JAMES MONTGOMERY

Angels from The Realms of glory,
Wing your flight o'er all the earth;
Ye who sang creation's story,
Now proclaim Messiah's birth:
Come and worship, Come and worship,
Worship Christ, the newborn king!

Shepherds, in the fields abiding,
Watching o'er your flocks by night,
God with man is now residing,
Yonder shines the infant Light:
Come and worship, Come and worship,
Worship Christ, the newborn king!

Sages, leave your contemplations,
Brighter visions beam afar;
Seek the great Desire of nations;
Ye have seen His natal star:
Come and worship, Come and worship,
Worship Christ, the newborn king!

O Holy Night

JOHN SULLIVAN DWIGHT

O holy night!
The stars are brightly shining,
It is the night
Of the dear savior's birth.

Long lay the world
in sin and error pining,
Till He appeared
and the soul felt His worth.

A thrill of hope
the weary world rejoices,
For yonder breaks
a new and glorious morn.

Fall on your knees
O hear the angel voices,
O night divine,
O night when Christ was born.

O night divine
O night,
O night divine.

Psalm for Christmas Day

THOMAS PESTEL

Fairest of morning lights appear,
    Thou blest and gaudy day,
On which was born our Saviour dear;
    Arise and come away!

This day prevents his day of doom;
    His mercy now is nigh;
The mighty God of love is come,
    The dayspring from on high!

Behold the great Creator makes
    Himself a house of clay,
A robe of virgin-flesh he takes
    Which he will wear for aye.

Hark, hark, the wise eternal Word
    Like a weak infant cries:

In form of servant is the Lord,
And God in cradle lies.

This wonder struck the world amazed,
It shook the starry frame;
Squadrons of spirits stood and gazed,
Then down in troops they came.

Glad shepherds ran to view this sight;
A quire of angels sings;
And eastern sages with delight
Adore this King of kings.

Join them all hearts that are not stone,
And all our voices prove,
To celebrate this holy one,
The God of peace and love.

New Prince, New Pomp

ROBERT SOUTHWELL

Behold a silly tender babe
    In freezing winter night
In homely manger trembling lies:
    Alas! a piteous sight.

The inns are full; no man will yield
    This little pilgrim bed;
But forced he is with silly beasts
    In crib to shroud his head.

Despise not him for lying there;
    First what he is inquire:
An orient pearl is often found
    In depth of dirty mire.

Weigh not his crib, his wooden dish,
    Nor beasts that by him feed;

Weigh not his mother's poor attire,
　　Nor Joseph's simple weed.

This stable is a Prince's court,
　　This crib his chair of state,
The beasts are parcel of his pomp,
The wooden dish his plate.

The persons in that poor attire
　　His royal liveries wear;
The Prince himself is come from heaven.
　　This pomp is prizèd there.

With joy approach, O Christian wight,
　　Do homage to thy King;
And highly praise this humble pomp
　　Which he from heaven doth bring.

A Carol

LISETTE WOODWORTH REESE

Mary the Mother
   Sang to her Son,
In a Bethlehem shed
   When the light was done

"Jesus, Jesus,
   Little son, sleep:
The tall Kings are gone,
   The lads with the sheep.

"Jesus, Jesus,
   My bosom is warm;
And Joseph and I
   Will keep You from harm."

On the Morning of Christ's Nativity

JOHN MILTON

This is the month, and this the happy morn,
Wherein the Son of Heaven's eternal king,
Of wedded Maid and Virgin Mother born,
Our great redemption from above did bring;
For so the holy sages once did sing,
    That he our deadly forfeit should release,
And with his Father work us a perpetual peace.

That glorious form, that light unsufferable,
And that far-beaming blaze of majesty,
Wherewith he wont at Heaven's high council-table
To sit the midst of Trinal Unity,
He laid aside; and here with us to be,
    Forsook the courts of everlasting day,
And chose with us a darksome house of mortal clay.

Say, Heavenly Muse, shall not thy sacred vein
Afford a present to the infant God?
Hast thou no verse, no hymn, or solemn strain,
To welcome him to this his new abode,
Now while the Heaven, by the sun's team untrod,
     Hath took no print of the approaching light,
And all the spangled host keep watch in squadrons bright?

See how from far upon the eastern road
The star-led wizards haste with odors sweet!
O run, prevent them with thy humble ode,
And lay it lowly at his blessed feet;
Have thou the honor first thy Lord to greet,
     And join they voice unto the angel choir,
From out his secret altar touched with hallowed fire.

The Hymn

It was the winter wild
While the Heaven-born child
     All meanly wrapped in the rude manger lies;
Nature in awe to him
Had doffed her gaudy trim,
     With her great Master so to sympathize;

It was no season then for her
To wanton with the sun, her lusty paramour.

Only with speeches fair
She woos the gentle air
    To hide her guilty front with innocent snow,
And on her naked shame,
Pollute with sinful blame,
    The saintly veil of maiden white to throw,
Confounded, that her Maker's eyes
Should look so near upon her foul deformities.

But her fears to cease,
Sent down the meek-eyed Peace;
    She, crowned with olive green, came softly sliding
Down through the turning sphere,
His ready harbinger,
    With turtle wing the amorous clouds dividing,
And waving wide her myrtle wand,
She strikes a universal peace through sea and land.

No war or battle's sound
Was heard the world around:
    The idle spear and shield were high uphung;
The hooked chariot stood

Unstained with hostile blood;
    The trumpet spake not to the armed throng;
And kings sat still with awful eye,
As if they surely knew their sovran Lord was by.

But peaceful was the night
Wherein the Prince of Light
    His reign of peace upon the earth began:
The winds with wonder whist,
Smoothly the waters kissed,
    Whispering new joys to the mild ocëan,
Who now hath quite forgot to rave,
While birds of calm sit brooding on the charmed wave.

The starts with deep amaze
Stand fixed in steadfast gaze,
    Bending one way their precious influence,
And will not take their flight
For all the morning light,
    Or Lucifer that often warned them thence;
But in their glimmering orbs did glow,
Until their Lord himself bespake, and bid them go.

And though the shady gloom
Had given day her room,
    The sun himself withheld his wonted speed,

And hid his head for shame,
As his inferior flame
    The new-enlightened world no more should need;
He saw a greater sun appear
Than his bright throne or burning axletree could bear.

The shepherds on the lawn,
Or ere the point of dawn,
    Sat simply chatting in a rustic row;
Full little thought they than
That the mighty Pan
    Was kindly come to live with them below;
Perhaps their loves, or else their sheep,
Was all that did their silly thoughts so busy keep.

When such music sweet
Their hearts and ears did greet,
    As never was by mortal finger strook,
Divinely warbled voice
Answering the stringed noise,
    As all their souls in blissful rapture took;
The air, such pleasure loth to lose,
With thousand echoes still prolongs each heavenly close.

Nature that heard such sound
Beneath the hollow round

Of Cynthia's seat, the airy region thrilling,
Now was almost won
To think her part was done,
    And that her reign had here its last fulfilling;
She knew such harmony alone
Could hold all Heaven and Earth in happier union.

At last surrounds their sight
A globe of circular light,
    That with long beams the shame-faced Night arrayed;
The helmed Cherubim
And sworded Seraphim
    Are seen in glittering ranks with wings displayed,
Harping in loud and solemn choir,
With unexpressive notes to Heaven's new-born Heir.

Such music (as 'tis said)
Before was never made,
    But when of old the sons of morning sung,
While the Creator great
His constellations set,
    And the well-balanced world on hinges hung,
And cast the dark foundations deep,
And bid the weltering waves their oozy channel keep.

Ring out, ye crystal spheres,
Once bless our human ears
    (If ye have power to touch our senses so),
And let your silver chime
Move in melodious time,
    And let the bass of Heaven's deep organ blow;
And with your ninefold harmony
Make up full consort to the angelic symphony.

For if such holy song
Enwrap our fancy long,
    Time will run back and fetch the age of gold,
And speckled Vanity
Will sicken soon and die,
    And leprous Sin will melt from earthly mold,
And Hell itself will pass away,
And leave her dolorous mansions to the peering day.

Yea, Truth and Justice then
Will down return to men,
    Orbed in a rainbow; and, like glories wearing,
Mercy will sit between,
Throned in celestial sheen,
    With radiant feet the tissued clouds down steering;
And Heaven, as at some festival,

Will open wide the gates of her high palace hall.
But wisest Fate says no,
This must not yet be so;
      The Babe lies yet in smiling infancy,
That on the bitter cross
Must redeem our loss,
      So both himself and us to glorify;
Yet first to those ychained in sleep,
The wakeful trump of doom must thunder through the deep,

With such a horrid clang
As on Mount Sinai rang
      While the red fire and smoldering clouds outbrake:
The aged Earth aghast
With terror of that blast,
      Shall from the surface to the center shake,
When at the world's last session
The dreadful Judge in middle air shall spread his throne.

And then at last our bliss
Full and perfect is,
      But now begins; for from this happy day
The old Dragon under ground,
In straiter limits bound,
      Not half so far casts his usurped sway,

And, wroth to see his kingdom fail,
Swinges the scaly horror of his folded tail.

The oracles are dumb,
No voice or hideous hum
    Runs through the arched roof in words deceiving.
Apollo from his shrine
Can no more divine,
    With hollow shriek the steep of Delphos leaving.
No nightly trance or breathed spell
Inspires the pale-eyed priest from the prophetic cell.

The lonely mountains o'er,
And the resounding shore,
    A voice of weeping heard, and loud lament;
From haunted spring and dale,
Edged with poplar pale,
    The parting Genius is with sighing sent;
With flower-inwoven tresses torn
The nymphs in twilight shade of tangled thickets mourn.

In consecrated earth,
And on the holy hearth,
    The Lars and Lemures moan with midnight plaint;
In urns and altars round,

A drear and dying sound
    Affrights the flamens at their service quaint;
And the chill marble seems to sweat,
While each peculiar power forgoes his wonted seat.

Peor and Baalim
Forsake their temples dim,
    With that twice-battered god of Palestine;
And mooned Ashtaroth,
Heaven's queen and mother both,
    Now sits not girt with tapers' holy shine;
The Libyc Hammon shrinks his horn,
In vain the Tyrian maids their wounded Thammuz mourn.

And sullen Moloch, fled,
Hath left in shadows dread
    His burning idol all of blackest hue;
In vain with cymbals' ring
They call the grisly king,
    In dismal dance about the furnace blue;
The brutish gods of Nile as fast,
Isis and Orus, and the dog Anubis, haste.

Nor is Osiris seen
In Memphian grove or green,

Trampling the unshowered grass with lowings loud;
Nor can he be at rest
Within his sacred chest,
Nought but profoundest Hell can be his shroud;
In vain with timbreled anthems dark
The sable-stoled sorcerers bear his worshiped ark.

He feels from Juda's land
The dreaded Infant's hand,
The rays of Bethlehem blink his dusky eyn;
Nor all the gods beside
Longer dare abide,
Not Typhon huge ending in snaky twine:
Our Babe, to show his Godhead true,
Can in his swaddling bands control the damned crew.

So when the sun in bed,
Curtained with cloudy red,
Pillows his chin upon and orient wave,
The flocking shadows pale
Troop to the infernal jail;
Each fettered ghost slips to his several grave;
And the yellow-skirted fays
Fly after the night-steeds, leaving their moon-loved maze.

But see, the Virgin blest
Hath laid her Babe to rest.
 Time is our tedious song should here have ending;
Heaven's youngest-teemed star
Hath fixed her polished car,
 Her sleeping Lord with handmaid lamp attending;
And all about the courtly stable
Bright-harnessed angels sit in order serviceable.

A Christmas Carol

CHRISTINA ROSSETTI

In the bleak mid-winter
 Frosty wind made moan,
Earth stood hard as iron,
 Water like a stone;
Snow had fallen, snow on snow,
 Snow on snow,
In the bleak mid-winter
 Long ago.

Our God, Heaven cannot hold Him
 Nor earth sustain;
Heaven and earth shall flee away
 When He comes to reign:
In the bleak mid-winter
 A stable-place sufficed
The Lord God Almighty
 Jesus Christ.

Enough for Him, whom cherubim
    Worship night and day,
A breastful of milk
    And a mangerful of hay;
Enough for Him, whom angels
    Fall down before,
The ox and ass and camel
    Which adore.

Angels and archangels
    May have gathered there,
Cherubim and seraphim
    Thronged the air;
But only His mother
    In her maiden bliss
Worshipped the Beloved
    With a kiss.

What can I give Him
    Poor as I am?
If I were a shepherd
    I would bring a lamb,
If I were a Wise Man
    I would do my part,—
Yet what I can I give Him,
    Give my heart.

Christmas Morning

ELIZABETH MADOX ROBERTS

If Bethlehem were here today,
Or this were very long ago,
There wouldn't be a winter time
Nor any cold or snow.

I'd run out through the garden gate,
And down along the pasture walk;
And off beside the cattle barns
I'd hear a kind of gentle talk.

I'd move the heavy iron chain
And pull away the wooden pin;
I'd push the door a little bit
And tiptoe very softly in.

The pigeons and the yellow hens
And all the cows would stand away;
Their eyes would open wide to see
A lady in the manger hay,

If there were very long ago
And Bethlehem were here today.

And mother held my hand and smiled—
I mean the lady would—and she
Would take the woolly blankets off
Her little boy so I could see.

His shut-up eyes would be asleep,
And he would look like our John,
And he would be all crumpled too,
And have a pinkish color on.

I'd watch his breath go in and out.
His little clothes would all be white.
I'd slip my finger in his hand
To feel how he could hold it tight.

And she would smile and say, "Take care,"
The mother, Mary, would, "Take care";
And I would kiss his little hand
And touch his hair

While Mary put the blankets back
The gentle talk would soon begin.
And when I'd tiptoe softly out
I'd meet the wise men going in.

A Christmas Carol
for Children

MARTIN LUTHER

Good news from heaven the angels bring,
Glad tidings to the earth they sing:
To us this day a child is given,
To crown us with the joy of heaven.

This is the Christ, our God and Lord,
Who in all need shall aid afford:
He will Himself our Saviour be,
From sin and sorrow set us free.

To us that blessedness He brings,
Which from the Father's bounty springs:
That in the heavenly realm we may
With Him enjoy eternal day.

All hail, Thou noble Guest, this morn,
Whose love did not the sinner scorn!

In my distress Thou cam'st to me:
What thanks shall I return to Thee?

Were earth a thousand times as fair,
Beset with gold and jewels rare,
She yet were far too poor to be
A narrow cradle, Lord, for Thee.

Ah, dearest Jesus, Holy Child!
Make Thee a bed, soft, undefiled,
Within my heart, that it may be
A quiet chamber kept for Thee.

Praise God upon His heavenly throne,
Who gave to us His only Son:
For this His hosts, on joyful wing,
A blest New Year of mercy sing.

No Sweeter Thing

ADELAIDE LOVE

Life holds no sweeter thing than this—to teach
A little child the tale most loved on earth
And watch the wonder deepen in his eyes
The while you tell him of the Christ Child's birth;

The while you tell of shepherds and a song,
Of gentle drowsy beasts and fragrant hay
On which that starlit night in Bethlehem
God's tiny Son and His young mother lay.

Life holds no sweeter thing that this—to tell
A little child, while Christmas candles glow,
The story of a Babe whose humble birth
Became the loveliest of truths we know.

Choir-Boys on Christmas Eve

LOUISE TOWNSEND NICHOLL

"Then sleep, Thou little Child." Thus, sweet and high,
The choir-boys sang, on Christmas Eve when men,
With dim-lit manger and with lullaby,
Pretend that Jesus is a child again.
Like candles, flickering soft, their voices went,
Or any light which is not of the sun;
Like sound whose large vibrations have been spent,
Or pale-gold texture all too thinly spun.
A woman's voice without her joy and fear
The tiny boys wove sheerly to and fro—
No woman could have sung so light and clear
The crooning words which only women know.
Mary must wonder and, remembering, weep
To hear these babies sing Her Child to sleep.

Good Christian Men, Rejoice

TRADITIONAL GERMAN CAROL

Good Christian men, rejoice,
With heart and soul and voice;
Give ye heed to what we say; News! News!
Jesus Christ is born today!
Ox and ass before Him bow,
And he is in the manger now;
Christ is born today!
Christ is born today!

Good Christian men, rejoice,
With heart and soul and voice;
Now ye hear of endless bliss; Joy! Joy!
Jesus Christ was born for this!
He hath op'n'd the heavenly door,
And man is blessèd evermore.
Christ was born for this,
Christ was born for this!

Good Christian men, rejoice,
With heart and soul and voice;
Now ye need not fear the grave; Peace! Peace!
Jesus Christ was born to save!
Calls you one and calls you all,
To gain his everlasting hall.
Christ was born to save,
Christ was born to save!

O Come
Little Children

JOHANN A.P. SCHULZ

O Come, little children, from cot and from hall,
O Come to the manger in Bethlehem's stall.
There meekly He lieth, the heavenly Child,
So poor and so humble, so sweet and so mild.

The hay is His pillow, the manger His bed,
The beasts stand in wonder to gaze on His head,
Yet there is where He lieth, so weak and so poor,
Come shepherds and wise men to kneel at His door.

Now "Glory to God!" sing the angels on high,
And "Peace upon earth!" heav'nly voices reply.
Then come, little children, and join in the lay
That gladdened the world on that first Christmas Day.

Silent Night, Holy Night

JOSEPH MOHR

Silent Night, Holy Night!
All is calm, all is bright,
'Round yon virgin mother and child!
Holy Infant, so tender and mild,
Sleep in heavenly peace,
Sleep in heavenly peace.

Silent Night, Holy Night!
Shepherds quake at the sight,
Glories stream from heaven afar,
Heav'nly hosts sing Alleluia;
Christ, the saviour is born.
Christ, the saviour is born.

Silent Night, Holy Night!
Son of God, love's pure light,
Radiant beams from thy holy face,

With the dawn of redeeming grace,
Jesus, Lord, at thy birth.
Jesus, Lord, at thy birth.

Silent Night, Holy Night!
Wondrous Star, lend thy light,
With the angels let us sing,
Allelulia to our King,
Christ, the Saviour is born,
Christ, the Saviour is born.

The Priceless Gift of Christmas

HELEN STEINER RICE

The priceless gift of Christmas
Is meant just for the heart,
And we receive it only
When we become a part
Of the kingdom and the glory
Which is ours to freely take,
For God sent the holy Christ Child
At Christmas for our sake
So man might come to know Him
And feel His presence near
And see the many miracles
Performed when He was here...
And the priceless gift of Christmas
Is within the reach of all,
The rich, the poor, the young and old,
The greatest and the small...

So take His priceless gift of love—
Reach out and you receive,
And the only payment that God asks
Is just that you believe.

The Glory of Christmas

LAVERNE RILEY O'BRIEN

Give thanks to the baby asleep in the hay,
For it's Jesus who gave us our first Christmas Day.
A king in disguise, God sent Him to men,
Revealed to our hearts, He comes again.

Lord of the galaxies as well as our earth,
A hymn of the Universe celebrates His birth.
He gives us His Spirit, His kingdom's within,
His peace can be ours by believing in Him.

His truth is a flame that ignites young souls,
He is comfort to men for whom the bell tolls,
He restores an image both marred and grown dim,
He's a constant wonder to those who love Him.

As we wrap up our presents to give them away,
We do this because of that first Christmas Day,
When the Lord of all glory and beauty and wealth
Came to earth as a Baby to give us Himself.

Go Tell It on the Mountain

TRADITIONAL AFRICAN AMERICAN SPIRITUAL

When I was a learner,
I sought night and day,
I asked the Lord to aid me
And He showed me the way.

Go tell it on the mountain
Over the hills and everywhere
Go till it on the mountain
That Jesus Christ is born.

While shepherds kept their watching
O'er silent flocks by night.
Behold, throughout the heavens
There shone a holy light.

Go tell it on the mountain
Over the hills and everywhere

Go till it on the mountain
That Jesus Christ is born.

The shepherds feared and trembled,
When, lo, above the earth
Rang out the angels' chorus,
That hailed our Saviour's birth

Go tell it on the mountain
Over the hills and everywhere
Go till it on the mountain
That Jesus Christ is born.

Down in a lowly manger,
Our humble Christ was born.
And God sent us salvation
That blessed Christmas morn.

Go tell it on the mountain
Over the hills and everywhere
Go till it on the mountain
That Jesus Christ is born.

The Hallowed Season

WILLIAM SHAKESPEARE

From "Hamlet"

Some say that ever 'gainst that season comes
Wherein our Saviour's birth is celebrated,
The bird of dawning singeth all night long:
And then, they say, no spirit dare stir abroad,
The nights are wholesome, then no planets strike,
No fairy takes nor witch hath power to charm,
So hallow'd and so gracious is the time.

Carol of the Field Mice

KENNETH GRAHAME

Villagers all, this frosty tide,
Let you doors swing open wide,
Though wind may follow, and snow beside,
Yet draw us in by your fire to hide;
 Joy shall be yours in the morning!

Here we stand in the cold and the sleet,
Blowing fingers and stamping feet,
Come from far away you to greet—
You by the fire and we in the street—
 Bidding you joy in the morning!

For ere one half of the night was gone,
Sudden a star has led us on,
Raining bliss and benison—
Bliss to-morrow and more anon,
 Joy for every morning!

Goodman Joseph toiled through the snow—
Saw the star o'er a stable low;
Mary she might not further go—
Welcome thatch, and litter below!
    Joy was hers in the morning!

And then they heard the angels tell
"Who were the first to cry Nowell?
Animals all, as it befell,
In the stable where they did dwell!
    Joy shall be theirs in the morning!"

Joy to the World

ISAAC WATTS

Joy to the world! The Lord is come.
Let Earth receive her King.
Let ev'ry heart prepare Him room,
And Heav'n and Nature sing,
And Heav'n and Nature sing,
And Heav'n, and Heav'n and Nature sing.

Joy to the world! The Savior reigns.
Let men their songs employ,
While fields and floods, rocks, hills, and plains
Repeat the sounding joy,
Repeat the sounding joy,
Repeat, repeat the sounding joy.

He rules the world with truth and grace
And makes the nations prove
The glories of His righteousness
And wonders of His love,
And wonders of His love,
And wonders, wonders of His love.

THE MERRY SEASON

Hymn for
Christmas Day

JOHN BYROM

Christians awake, salute the happy Morn,
Whereon the Saviour of the World was born;
Rise, to adore the Mystery of Love,
Which Hosts of Angels chanted from above:
With them the joyful Tidings first begun
Of God incarnate, and the Virgin's Son:
Then to the watchful Shepherds it was told,
Who heard th' Angelic Herald's Voice—Behold!
I bring good Tidings of a Saviour's Birth
To you, and all the Nations upon Earth;
This Day hath God fulfill'd his promis'd Word;
This Day is born a Saviour, Christ, the Lord:
In David's City, Shepherds, ye shall find
The long foretold Redeemer of Mankind;
Wrapt up in swaddling Cloaths, the Babe divine
Lies in a Manger; this shall be your Sign.
He spake, and straightway the Celestial Choir,

In Hymns of Joy, unknown before, conspire:
The Praises of redeeming Love they sung,
And Heav'ns whole Orb with Hallelujahs rung:
God's highest Glory was their Anthem still;
Peace upon Earth, and mutual Good-will.
To Bethlehem straight th' enlightened Shepherds ran,
To see the Wonder God had wrought for Man;
And found, with Joseph and the blessed Maid,
Her Son, the Saviour, in a Manger laid.
Amaz'd, the wond'rous Story they proclaim;
The first Apostles of his Infant Fame:
While Mary keeps, and ponders in her Heart,
The heav'nly Vision, which the Swains impart;
They to their Flocks, still praising God, return,
And their glad Hearts within their Bosoms burn.
Let us, like these good Shepherds then, employ
Our grateful Voices to proclaim the Joy:
Like Mary, let us ponder in our Mind
God's wond'rous Love in saving lost Mankind;
Artless, and watchful, as these favour'd Swains,
While Virgin Meekness in the Heart remains:
Trace we the Babe, who has retriev'd our Loss,
From his poor Manger to his bitter Cross;
Trading his Steps, assisted by his Grace,
'Till Man's first heav'nly State again takes Place:

Then may we hope, th' Angelic Thrones among,
To sing, redeem'd, a glad triumphal Song:
He that was born, upon this joyful Day,
Around us all, his Glory shall display;
Sav'd by his Love, incessant we shall sing
Of Angels, and of Angel-Men, the King.

The Most Wonderful Time of the Year

EDDIE POLA AND GEORGE WYLE

It's the most wonderful time of the year,
with the kids jingle belling
and everyone telling you,
"Be of good cheer."
It's the most wonderful time of the year.

It's the happiest season of all,
with those holiday greetings
and gay happy meetings,
when friends come to call.
It's the most wonderful time of the year.

It's the most wonderful time of the year.
There'll be much mistletoeing
and hearts will be glowing
when loved ones are near.
It's the most wonderful time of the year.

It's the happiest season of all.
There'll be parties for hosting,
marshmallows for toasting
and caroling out in the snow.
There'll be scary ghost stories
and tales and glories or Christmases
long, long ago.
It's the most wonderful time of the year.

It's the most wonderful time of the year.
There'll be much mistletoeing
and hearts will be glowing
when loved ones are near.

It's the most wonderful time,
it's the most wonderful time,
it's the most wonderful time of the year.

Christmas Morning

JOAQUIN MILLER

The bells ring clear as bugle note;
Sweet song is filling every throat;
    'Tis welcome Christmas morning!
O, never yet was morn so fair;
Such silent music in the air;
    'Tis Merry Christmas morning!

Dear day of all days in the year;
Dear day of song, goodwill and cheer;
    'Tis golden Christmas morning!
The hope, the faith, the love that is,
The peace, the holy promises;
    'Tis glorious Christmas morning!

Christmas Everywhere

PHILLIPS BROOKS

Everywhere, everywhere, Christmas tonight!
Christmas in land of fir-tree and pine,
Christmas in lands of palm-tree and vine,
Christmas where snow peaks stand solemn and white,
Christmas where cornfields lie sunny and bright.
Everywhere, everywhere, Christmas tonight!

Christmas where children are hopeful and gay,
Christmas where old men are patient and gray,
Christmas where peace, like a dove in his flight,
Broods o're brave men in the thick of the fight;
Everywhere, everywhere, Christmas tonight!

For the Christ-child who comes is the Master of all;
No palace too great, no cottage too small.
The Angels who welcome Him sing from the height,
"In the city of David, a King in His might."
Everywhere, everywhere, Christmas tonight.

Then let every heart keep its Christmas within.
Christ's pity for sorrow, Christ's hatred for sin,
Christ's care for the weakest, Christ's courage for right,
Christ's dread for darkness, Christ's love of the light,
Everywhere, everywhere, Christmas tonight!

So the stars of the midnight which compass us round
Shall see a strange glory, and hear a sweet sound,
And cry, "Look! the earth is aflame with delight,
O sons of the morning, rejoice at the sight."
Everywhere, everywhere, Christmas tonight.

Christmas Snowflakes

SASHA ISABELLA ALEXANDER

Oh to be a snowflake, born on Christmas night,
Soaring through the air, floating with delight,
Down, down, down below. Listen. Don't you hear?
The joyful chimes of Christmas, ringing out good cheer.

Dancing high, we gracefully sway
As we dance to a winter's night ballet.
Sometimes fast, then maybe slow,
We dance our way to the town below.

See the children, filled with glee,
Decorating their beloved Christmas tree,
Baking cookies for Santa Claus,
Wrapping presents, then they pause—

Up the stairs and into beds,
Where they can rest their little heads!
We guard their windows through the night
To see their joy at morning's light.

Deck the Halls

TRADITIONAL WELSH CAROL

Deck the halls with boughs of holly,
Fa la la la la la la la la.
'Tis the season to be jolly,
Fa la la la la la la la la.
Don we now our gay apparel,
Fa la la la la la la la la.
Troll the ancient Yuletide carol,
Fa la la la la la la la la.

See the blazing Yule before us,
Fa la la la la la la la la.
Strike the harp and join the chorus,
Fa la la la la la la la la.
Follow me in merry measure,
Fa la la la la la la la la.
While I tell of Yuletide treasure,
Fa la la la la la la la la.

Fast away the old year passes,
Fa la la la la la la la la.
Hail the new, ye lads and lasses,
Fa la la la la la la la la.
Sing we joyous all together,
Fa la la la la la la la la.
Heedless of the wind and weather,
Fa la la la la la la la la.

Deck the halls with boughs of holly,
Fa la la la la la la la la.

The Holly and the Ivy

TRADITIONAL ENGLISH CAROL

The holly and the ivy,
When they are both full grown,
Of all the trees that are in the wood,
The holly bears the crown.

O, the rising of the sun,
And the running of the deer,
The playing of the merry organ,
Sweet singing in the choir.

The holly wears a blossom
As white as the lily flower;
And Mary bore sweet Jesus Christ
To be our sweet Saviour.

O, the rising of the sun,
And the running of the deer,
The playing of the merry organ,
Sweet singing in the choir.

The holly bears a berry
As red as any blood;
And Mary bore sweet Jesus Christ
To do poor sinners good.

O, the rising of the sun,
And the running of the deer,
The playing of the merry organ,
Sweet singing in the choir.

The holly bears a prickle
As sharp as any thorn;
And Mary bore sweet Jesus Christ
On Christmas Day in the morn.

O, the rising of the sun,
And the running of the deer,
The playing of the merry organ,
Sweet singing in the choir.

The holly bears a bark
As bitter as any gall;
And Mary bore sweet Jesus Christ
For to redeem us all.

O, the rising of the sun,
And the running of the deer,

The playing of the merry organ,
Sweet singing in the choir.

The holly and the ivy
Now both are full well grown,
Of all the trees that are in the wood,
The holly bears the crown.

O, the rising of the sun,
And the running of the deer,
The playing of the merry organ,
Sweet singing in the choir.

Christmas Time Is Here

LEE MENDELSON AND VINCE GUARALDI

Christmas time is here,
happiness and cheer.
Fun for all that children call
their favorite time of year

Snowflakes in the air,
carols every-where.
Olden times and ancient rhymes
of love and dreams to share.

Sleigh bells in the air,
beauty every-where.
Yuletide by the fireside
and joyful memories there.

Christmas time is here,
we'll be drawing near.
Oh that we could always see
such spirit through the year.

A Christmas Carol

AUTHOR UNKNOWN

The other night
I saw a light!
   A star as bright as day!
And ever among
A maiden sung:
   "By-by, baby, lullay."

This virgin clear
Who had no peer
   Unto her son did say,
"I pray thee, son,
Grant me a boon
   To sing by-by, lullay.

"Let child or man,
Whoever can
   Be merry on this day,
And blessings bring—
So I shall sing
   'By-by, baby, lullay.'"

Now Is the Time of Cristmas

JAMES RYMAN

Make we mery, both more and lass,
For now is the time of Cristymas.

Let no man cum into this hall,
Grome, page, nor yet marshàll,
But that some sport he bring withal,
    For now is the time of Cristmas.

If that he say he can not sing,
Some other sport then let him bring
That it may please at this festing,
    For now is the time of Cristmas.

If he say he can nought do,
Then for my love ask him no mo,
But to the stokkes then let him go,
    For now is the time of Cristmas.

The Love
That Lives

Every child on earth is holy,
Every crib is a manger lowly,
Every home is a stable dim,
Every kind word is a hymn,
Every star is God's own gem,
And every town is Bethlehem,
For Christ is born and born again,
When His love lives in hearts of men.

The Christmas Song
(Chestnuts Roasting on An Open Fire)

MEL TORME AND ROBERT WELLS

Chestnuts roasting on an open fire,
Jack Frost nipping at your nose,
Yuletide carols being sung by a choir
and folks dressed up like Eskimos.

Everybody knows a turkey and some mistletoe
help to make the season bright.
Tiny tots with their eyes all aglow
will find it hard to sleep tonight.

They know that Santa's on his way;
he's loaded lots of toys and goodies on his sleigh,
and every mother's child is gonna spy
to see if reindeer really know how to fly.

And so I'm offering this simply phrase
to kids from one to ninety-two.
Although it's been said many times, many ways,
"Merry Christmas to you."

Masters in This Hall

WILLIAM MORRIS

Masters in this hall,
Hear ye news today,
Brought from over-sea
And ever I you pray.

Nowell, Nowell, Nowell!
Nowell sing we clear!
Holpen are all folk on earth
born is God's Son so dear;

Nowell, Nowell, Nowell!
Nowell sing we loud!
God today hath all folk raised
And cast a-down the proud.

Then to Bethl'em town
We went two and two;
In a sorry place
We heard the oxen low:

Nowell, Nowell, Nowell!
Nowell sing we clear!
Holpen are all folk on earth
born is God's Son so dear;

Nowell, Nowell, Nowell!
Nowell sing we loud!
God today hath all folk raised
And cast a-down the proud.

Ox and ass Him know,
Kneeling on their knee,
Wond'rous joy had I
This little babe to see:

Nowell, Nowell, Nowell!
Nowell, sing we clear!
Holpen are all folk on earth
born is God's Son so dear;

Nowell, Nowell, Nowell!
Nowell sing we loud!
God today hath all folk raised
And cast a-down the proud.

This is Christ, the Lord,
Masters be ye glad!

Christmas is come in
And no folk should be sad.

Nowell, Nowell, Nowell!
Nowell, sing we clear!
Holpen are all folk on earth
born is God's Son so dear;

Nowell, Nowell, Nowell!
Nowell sing we loud!
God today hath all folk raised
And cast a-down the proud.

Pat-A-Pan

TRADITIONAL FRENCH CAROL

Willie, take your little drum
With your whistle, Robin come!
When we hear the fife and drum
Turelurelu pat-a-pat-a-pan
When we hear the fife and drum
Christmas should be frolicsome

Thus the men of olden days
Loved the King of kings to praise
When they hear the fife and drum
Turelurelu pat-a-pat-a-pan
When they hear the fife and drum
Sure our children won't be dumb

God and men are now become
More at one than fife and drum
When you hear the fife and drum
Turelurelu pat-a-pat-a-pan
When you hear the fife and drum
Dance and make the village hum!

Merry Christmas

LOUISA MAY ALCOTT

In the rush of early morning,
When the red burns through the gray,
And the wintry world lies waiting
For the glory of the day,

Then we hear a fitful rustling
Just without upon the stair,
See two small white phantoms coming,
Catch the gleam of sunny hair.

Are they Christmas fairies stealing
Rows of little socks to fill?
Are they angels floating hither
With their message of good-will?

What sweet spell are these elves weaving,
As like larks they chirp and sing?
Are these palms of peace from heaven
That these lovely spirits bring?

Rosy feet upon the threshold,
Eager faces peeping through,
With the first red ray of sunshine,
Chanting cherubs come in view:

Mistletoe and gleaming holly,
Symbols of a blessed day,
In their chubby hands they carry,
Streaming all along the way.

Well we know them, never weary
Of this innocent surprise;
Waiting, watching, listening always
With full hearts and tender eyes,

While out little household angels,
White and golden in the sun
Greet us with the sweet old welcome,—
"Merry Christmas, every one!"

We Need a Little Christmas

JERRY HERMAN

Haul out the holly
Put up the tree before my spirit falls again
Fill up the stocking
I may be rushing things, but deck the halls again now

For we need a little Christmas
Right this very minute
Candles in the window
Carols at the spinet

Yes, we need a little Christmas
Right this very minute
It hasn't snowed a single flurry
But Santa, dear, we're in a hurry

So climb down the chimney
Turn on the brightest string of lights I've ever seen
Slice up the fruitcake
It's time we hung some tinsel on that evergreen bough

For I've grown a little leaner
Grown a little colder
Grown a little sadder
Grown a little older
And I need a little angel
Sitting on my shoulder
Need a little Christmas now

For we need a little music
Need a little laughter
Need a little singing
Ringing through the rafter

And we need a little snappy
"Happy ever after"
Need a little Christmas now

All You That to Feasting and Mirth Are Inclined

AUTHOR UNKNOWN

All you that to feasting and mirth are inclined,
Come here is good news for to pleasure your mind,
Old Christmas is come for to keep open house,
He scorns to be guilty of starving a mouse:
Then come, boys, and welcome for diet the chief,
Plum-pudding, goose, capon, minced pies, and roast beef.
The holly and ivy about the walls wind
And show that we ought to our neighbors be kind,
Inviting each other for pastime and sport,
And where we best fare, there we most do resort;
We fail not of victuals, and that of the chief,
Plum-pudding, goose, capon, minced pies, and roast beef.
All travelers, as they do pass on their way,
At gentlemen's halls are invited to stay,
Themselves to refresh, and their horses to rest,
Since that he must be Old Christmas's guest;
Nay, the poor shall not want, but have for relief,
Plum-pudding, goose, capon, minced pies, and roast beef.

The Christmas Tree

EMMA LAZARUS

Crusted with silver, gemmed with stars of light,
  Topaz and ruby, emerald, sapphire, pearl,
The enchanted tree within a world of white
Uplifts her myriad crystal branches bright
  Against the pale blue skies. The keen winds whirl
Her globèd jewels on the sheeted snow,
That hard and pure as marble lies below.

Yet even the radiant fruitage falls,
  Touching the solid earth, it melts to air.
Gold-glimmering rings and clear, flame-hearted balls,—
These be the magic keys to elfin halls.
  The outstretched hands of greed are void and bare,
But elfin hands may clasp, elf eyes may see,
The mystic glories of the wondrous tree.

Lo, as beneath the silver boughs I stood,
  And watched the gleaming jewel in their heart,
Blue as a star, the subtle charm held good:

I touched and clasped a dropping diamond dart,
    And, rapt from all the snowy world apart,
Alone within the moist, green woods of May,
I wandered ere the middle hour of day.

And over me the magic tree outspread
    Her rustling branches like a silken tent;
An azure light the balmy heavens shed;
Rose-white with odorous bloom above my head,
    Scarce 'neath their burden soft the wreathed sprays bent.
Through them went singing birds, and once on high
Surely a blindfold, winged boy-god flew by.

In the cool shade two happy mortals stood
    And laughed, because the spring was in their veins,
Coursing like heavenly fire along their blood,
To see the sunbeams pierce the emerald wood,
    To head each other's voice, to catch the strains
Of sweet bird-carols in the tree-tops high;
And laughed like gods, who are not born to die.

A spirit murmured in mine ear unseen,
    "Rub well the dart thou holdest." I obeyed,
And all the tree was swathed in living green,
Veiled with hot, hazy sunshine, and between
    The ripe, dark leaves plump cherries white and red,

Swaying on slender stalks with every breeze,
Glowed like the gold fruits of Hesperides.

Once more I rubbed the talisman. There came
Once more a change: the rusty leaves outshone
With tints of bronze against a sky of flame,
Weird with strange light, the same yet not the same.
  But brief the glory, setting with the sun:
A fog-white wraith uprose to haunt the tree,
And shrill winds whistled through it drearily.

From out my hand the mystic arrow fell:
  Like dew it vanished, and I was aware
Of winter-tide and death. Ah, was it well,
Ye mocking elves, to weave this subtle spell,
  And break it thus, dissolving into air
The fairy fabric of my dream, and show
Life a brief vision melting with the snow?

Silver Bells

JAY LIVINGSTON AND RAY EVANS

Christmas makes you feel emotional.
it may bring parties or thoughts devotional.
What ever happens or what may be
here is what Christmas means to me.

City sidewalks, busy sidewalks
dressed in holiday style;
in the air there's a feeling
of Christmas.

Children laughing,
people passing,
meeting smile after smile,
and on every street corner you hear;

Silver bells, silver bells,
it's Christmas time in the city.
Ring-a-ling, hear them ring,
soon it will be Christmas Day.

Strings of street lights,
even stoplights
blink a bright red and green
as the shoppers rush home with their treasures

Hear the snow crunch,
see the kids bunch,
this is Santa's big scene,
and above all this bustle you hear:

Silver bells, silver bells,
it's Christmas time in the city.
Ring-a-ling, hear them ring,
soon it will be Christmas Day.

God Rest You Merry, Gentlemen

TRADITIONAL ENGLISH CAROL

God rest you merry, gentlemen,
  Let nothing you dismay,
Remember Christ our Saviour
  Was born on Christmas Day;
To save us all from Satan's power
  When we were gone astray.

O tidings of comfort and joy,
  comfort and joy;
O tidings of comfort and joy!

In Bethlehem in Jewry
This blessèd babe was born
And laid within a manger
Upon this blessèd morn;
The which his mother Mary
Nothing did take in scorn:

O tidings of comfort and joy,
    comfort and joy;
O tidings of comfort and joy!

From God our heavenly Father
A blessèd angel came.
And unto certain shepherds
Brought tidings of the same,
How that in Bethlehem was born
The Son of God by name:

O tidings of comfort and joy,
    comfort and joy;
O tidings of comfort and joy!

"Fear not," then said the angel,
"Let nothing you affright,
This day is born a Savior,
Of virtue, power, and might;
So frequently to vanquish all
The friends of Satan quite:"

O tidings of comfort and joy,
    comfort and joy;
O tidings of comfort and joy!

The shepherds at those tidings
Rejoicèd much in mind,
And left their flocks a-feeding,
In tempest, storm, and wind,
And went to Bethlehem straightway
This blessèd babe to find:

O tidings of comfort and joy,
    comfort and joy;
O tidings of comfort and joy!

But when to Bethlehem they came,
Whereat this infant lay
They found him in a manger,
Where oxen feed on hay;
His mother Mary kneeling,
Unto the Lord did pray:

O tidings of comfort and joy,
    comfort and joy;
O tidings of comfort and joy!

Now to the Lord sing praises,
All you within this place,
And with true love and brotherhood

Each other now embrace;
This holy tide of Christmas
All others doth deface:

O tidings of comfort and joy,
    comfort and joy;
O tidings of comfort and joy!

God bless the ruler of this house,
And send him long to reign,
And many a merry Christmas
May live to see again;
Among your friends and kindred
That live both far and near—
And God send you a happy new year, happy ne
And God send you a happy new year.

Christ Was Born on Christmas Day

TRADITIONAL GERMAN CAROL

Christ was born on Christmas Day,
Wreath the holly, twine the bay;
Christus natus hodie,
The Babe, the Son, the Holy One of Mary.

He is born to set us free,
He is born our Lord to be:
Ex Maria Virgine,
The God, the Lord, by all adored forever.

Let the bright red berries glow
Everywhere in goodly show:
Christus natus hodie,
The Babe, the Son, the Holy One of Mary.

Christian men, rejoice and sing
'Tis the birthday of a king:
Ex Maria Virgine,
The God, the Lord, by all adored forever.

O Christmas Tree

TRADITIONAL GERMAN CAROL

O Christmas tree, O Christmas tree,
You stand in verdant beauty!
O Christmas tree, O Christmas tree,
You stand in verdant beauty.
Your boughs so green in summer's glow
And do not fade in winters snow
O Christmas tree, O Christmas tree
You stand in verdant beauty.

O Christmas tree, O Christmas tree,
Of all the trees most lovely,
O Christmas tree, O Christmas tree,
Of all the trees most lovely,
Each year, you bring to me delight
Gleaming in the Christmas night.
O Christmas tree, O Christmas tree,
Of all the trees most lovely,

O Christmas tree, O Christmas tree,
Thy faith remains unchanging;
O Christmas tree, O Christmas tree,
Thy faith remains unchanging.
A symbol sent from God above,
Proclaiming Him the Lord of Love;
O Christmas tree, O Christmas tree,
Thy faith remains unchanging!

I Am Cristmas

JAMES RYMAN

Now have good day, now have good day!
I am Cristmas, and now I go my way.

Here have I dwelled with more and lass
From Halowtide till Candelmas,
And now must I from you hens pass;
    Now have good day!

I take my leve of king and knight,
And erl, baron, and lady bright;
To wilderness I must be dight;
    Now have good day!

And at the good lord of this hall
I take my leve, and of gestes all;
Me think I here Lent doth call;
    Now have good day!

And at every worthy officère,
Marshall, panter, and butlère,
I take my leve as for this yere;
    Now have good day!

Another yere I trust I shall
Make mery in this hall,
If rest and peace in England fall;
    Now have good day!

But oftentimes I have herd say
That he is loth to part away
That often biddeth 'Have good day!';
    Now have good day!

Now fare ye well, all in fere,
Now fare ye well for all this yere;
Yet for my sake make ye good chere;
    Now have good day!

Ceremonies for Candelmas

ROBERT HERRICK

Down with the rosemary and bays,
  Down with the mistletoe;
Instead of holly, now up-raise
  The green box, for show.

The holly hitherto did sway;
  Let box now domineer;
Until the dancing Easter-day,
On Easrer's eve appear.

Then youthful box, which now hath grace,
Your houses to renew;
Grown old, surrender must his place,
Unto the crispéd yew.

When yew is out, then birch comes in,
And many flowers beside;

Both of a fresh and fragrant kin
    To honor Whitsuntide.

Green rushes then, and sweetest bents,
    With cooler oaken boughs,
Come in for comely ornaments
    To re-adorn the house.

Thus times do shift; each thing his turn does hold;
New things succeed, as former things grow old.

Down with the rosemary, and so
Down with the bays and mistletoe;
Down with the holly, ivy, all,
Wherewith ye dressed the Christmas Hall:
That so the superstitious find
No one least branch there left behind:
For look how many leaves there be
Neglected, there (maids, trust to me)
So many goblins you shall see.

Christmas Pie

GEORGE WITHER

Lo! now is come our joyfull'st feast!
　　Let every man be jolly;
Each room with ivy leaves is dressed,
　　And every post with holly.
Now all our neighbours' chimneys smoke,
　　And Christmas blocks are burning;
Their ovens they with bakemeats choke,
　　And all their spits are turning.
Without the door let sorrow lie,
　　And if for cold it hap to die,
We'll bury it in a Christmas pie,
And ever more be merry.

Christmas
in a Village

Each house swept the day before,
And windows stuck with evergreens;
The snow is besomed from the door,
And comfort crowns the cottage scenes.
Gilt holly with its thorny pricks
And yew and box with berries small,
These deck the unused candlesticks,
And pictures hanging by the wall.

Neighbours resume their annual cheer,
Wishing with smiles and spirits high
Glad Christmas and a happy year
To every morning passer-by.
Milkmaids their Christmas journeys go
Accompanied with favoured swain,
And children pace the crumping snow
To taste their granny's cake again.

Hung with the ivy's veining bough,
The ash trees round the cottage farm
Are often stripped of branches now
The cottar's Christmas hearth to warm.
He swings and twists his hazel band,
And lops them off with sharpened hook,
And oft brings ivy in his hand,
To decorate the chimney hook...

The shepherd now no more afraid
Since custom doth the chance bestow
Starts up to kiss the giggling maid
Beneath the branch of mistletoe
That 'neath each cottage beam is seen
With pearl-like berries shining gay,
The shadow still of what hath been
Which fashion yearly fades away.

And singers too, a merry throng,
At early morn with simple skill
Yet imitate the angel's song
And chant their Christmas ditty still;
And 'mid the storm that dies and swells
By fits—in hummings softly steals
The music of the village bells
Ringing round their merry peals.

And when it's past, a merry crew
Bedecked in masks and ribbons gay,
The morris dance their sports renew
And act their winter evening play.
The clown turned king for penny praise
Storms with the actor's strut and swell,
And harlequin a laugh to raise
Wears his hunchback and tinkling bell.

And oft for pence and spicy ale
With winter nosegays pinned before,
The wassail singer tells her tale
And drawls her Christmas carols o'er,
While prentice boy with ruddy face
And rime-bepowdered dancing locks
From door to door with happy pace
Runs round to claim his Christmas box.

Ceremonies for Christmasse

ROBERT HERRICK

Come, bring with a noise,
My merrie merrie boyes,
The Christmas Log to the firing;
While my good Dame, she
Bids ye all be free;
And drink to your hearts desiring.

With the last yeeres brand
Light the new block, And
For good successe in his spending,
On your Psaltries play,
That sweet luck may
Come while the Log is a teending.

Drink now the strong Beere,
Cut the white loafe here,

The while the meat is a shredding
For the rare Mince-Pie;
And the Plums stand by
To fill the Paste that's a kneading.

Jingle Bells

JAMES S. PIERPONT

Dashing thro' the snow,
In a one-horse open sleigh;
O'er the fields we go,
Laughing all the way;
Bells on bob-tail ring
Making spirits bright;
What fun it is to ride and sing
A sleighing song to-night!

Jingle, bells! Jingle, bells!
Jingle all the way!
Oh! what fun it is to ride
In a one-horse open sleigh!
Jingle, bells! Jingle, bells!
Jingle all the way!
Oh! what fun it is to ride
In a one-horse open sleigh!

A day or two ago
I thought I'd take a ride,
And soon Miss Fannie Bright
Was seated by my side.
The horse was lean and lank;
Misfortune seem'd his lot;
He go into a drifted bank,
And we, we got up-sot.

Jingle, bells! Jingle, bells!
Jingle all the way!
Oh! what fun it is to ride
In a one-horse open sleigh!
Jingle, bells! Jingle, bells!
Jingle all the way!
Oh! what fun it is to ride
In a one-horse open sleigh!

Now the ground is white;
Go it while you're young;
Take the girls to-night,
And sing this sleighing song.
Just get a bob-tail'd bay,
Two-forty for his speed;
Then hitch him to an open sleigh,
And crack! you'll take the lead.

Jingle, bells! Jingle, bells!
Jingle all the way!
Oh! what fun it is to ride
In a one-horse open sleigh!
Jingle, bells! Jingle, bells!
Jingle all the way!
Oh! what fun it is to ride
In a one-horse open sleigh!

little tree

e. e. cummings

little tree
little silent Christmas tree
you are so little
you are more like a flower

who found you in the green forest
and were you very sorry to come away?
see... i will comfort you
because you smell so sweetly

i will kiss your cool bark
and hug you safe and tight
just as your mother would,
only don't be afraid

look... the spangles
that sleep all the year in a dark box

dreaming of being taken out and allowed to shine,
the balls the chains red and gold the fluffy threads,

put up your little arms
and i'll give them all to you to hold
every finger shall have its ring
and there won't be a single place dark or unhappy

then when you're quite dressed
you'll stand in the window for everyone to see
and how they'll stare!
oh but you'll be very proud

and my little sister and i will take hands
and looking up at our beautiful tree
we'll dance and sing
"Noel Noel"

Christmas Laughter

NIKKI GIOVANNI

My family is very small
Eleven of us
Three are over 80
Three are over 60
Three are over 50
Two of us are sons

Come Labor Day the quilts
are taken from the clean white sheets
in which they summered

We seldom have reason
and need no excuse
to polish the good silver
wash the tall stemmed glasses
and invite one another
into our homes

We win at Bid Whist
and lose at Canasta

and eat the lightest miniature Parker House rolls
and the world's best
five cheese macaroni and cheese

I grill the meat
Mommy boils the beans

Come first snow the apple cider
with nutmeg... cloves... cinnamon...
and just a hint of ginger
brews every game day and night

We have no problem
luring
Santa Claus
down
our chimney

He can't resist
The laughter

DEAR
SANTA

The Boy Who Laughed at Santa Claus

OGDEN NASH

In Baltimore there lived a boy.
He wasn't anybody's joy.
Although his name was Jabez Dawes,
His character was full of flaws.
In school he never led the classes,
He hid old ladies' reading glasses,
His mouth was open while he chewed,
And elbows to the table glued.
He stole the milk of hungry kittens,
And walked through doors marked No Admittance.
He said he acted thus because
There wasn't any Santa Claus.
Another trick that tickled Jabez
Was crying "Boo!" at little babies.
He brushed his teeth, they said in town,
Sideways instead of up and down.

Yet people pardoned every sin
And viewed his antics with a grin
Till they were told by Jabez Dawes,
"There isn't any Santa Claus!"
Deploring how he did behave,
His parents quickly sought their grave.
They hurried through the portals pearly,
And Jabez left the funeral early.
Like whooping cough, from child to child,
He sped to spread the rumor wild:
"Sure as my name is Jabez Dawes
There isn't any Santa Claus!"
Slunk like a weasel or a marten
Through nursery and kindergarten,
Whispering low to every tot,
"There isn't any, no, there's not!
No beard, no pipe, no scarlet clothes,
No twinkling eyes, no cherry nose,
No sleigh, and furthermore, by Jiminy,
Nobody coming down the chimney!"
The children wept all Christmas Eve
And Jabez chortled up his sleeve.
No infant dared to hang up his stocking
For fear of Jabez' ribald mocking.
He sprawled on his untidy bed,

Fresh malice dancing in his head,
When presently with scalp a-tingling,
Jabez heard a distant jingling;
He heard the crunch of sleigh and hoof
Crisply alighting on the roof.
What good to rise and bar the door?
A shower of soot was on the floor.
Jabez beheld, oh, awe of awes,
The fireplace full of Santa Claus!
Then Jabez fell upon his knees
With cries of "Don't," and "Pretty please."
He howled, "I don't know where you read it.
I swear some other fellow said it!"
"Jabez," replied the angry saint,
"It isn't I, it's you that ain't.
Although there *is* a Santa Claus,
There isn't any Jabez Dawes!"
Said Jabez then with impudent vim,
"Oh, yes there is; and I am him!
Your language don't scare me, it doesn't –"
And suddenly he found he wasn't!
From grinning feet to unkempt locks
Jabez became a jack-in-the-box,
An ugly toy in Santa's sack,
Mounting the flue on Santa's back.

The neighbors heard his mournful squeal;
They searched for him, but not with zeal.
No trace was found of Jabez Dawes,
Which led to thunderous applause,
And people drank a loving cup
And went and hung their stockings up.
All you who sneer at Santa Claus,
Beware the fate of Jabez Dawes,
The saucy boy who told the saint off;
The child who got him, licked his paint off.

Here Comes Santa Claus
(Right Down Santa Claus Lane)

GENE AUTRY AND OAKLEY HALDEMAN

Here comes Santa Claus! Here comes Santa Claus!
Right down Santa Claus Lane!
Vixen and Blitzen and all his reindeer
are pulling on the rein.

Bells are ringing, children singing,
all is merry and bright.
Hang your stockings and say your pray'rs,
'cause Santa Claus comes tonight.

Here comes Santa Claus! Here comes Santa Claus!
Right down Santa Claus Lane!
He's got a bag that is filled with toys
for the boys and girls again.

Hear those sleighbells jingle jangle,
what a beautiful sight.
Jump in bed, cover up your head,
'cause Santa Claus comes tonight.

Here comes Santa Claus! Here comes Santa Claus!
Right down Santa Claus Lane!
He doesn't care if you're rich or poor,
for he loves you just the same.

Santa knows that we're God's children;
that makes everything right.
Fill your hearts with a Christmas cheer,
'cause Santa Claus comes tonight.

Here comes Santa Claus! Here comes Santa Claus!
Right down Santa Claus Lane!
He'll come around when the chimes ring out;
then it's Christmas morn again.

Peace on earth will come to all
if we just follow the light.
Let's give thanks to the Lord above,
'cause Santa Claus comes tonight.

Kriss Kringle

THOMAS BAILEY ALDRICH

Just as the moon was fading mid her misty rings,
And every stocking was stuffed wit childhood's precious things,
Old Kriss Kringle looked around, and saw on the elm-tree bough,
High-hung, an oriole's nest, silent and empty now.

"Quite like a stocking," he laughed, "pinned up there on the tree!
Little I thought the birds expected a present from me!"
Then old Kriss Kringle, who loves a joke as well as the best,
Dropped a handful of flakes in the oriole's empty nest.

Christmas Island

KATHERINE LEE BATES

Fringed with coral, floored with lava,
Three-score leagues to south of Java,
So is Christmas Island charted
By geographers blind-hearted,
—Just a dot, by their dull notion,
On the burning Indian Ocean;
Merely a refreshment station
For the birds in long migration;
Its pomegranates, custard-apples
That the dancing sunshine dapples,
Cocoanuts with milky hollows
Only feast wing-weary swallows
Or the tropic fowl there dwelling.
Don't believe a word they're telling!
Christmas Island, though it seem land,
Is a floating bit of dreamland
Gone adrift from childhood, planted
By the winds with seeds enchanted,

Seeds of candied plum and cherry;
Here the Christmas Saints make merry.

Even saints must have vacation;
So they chose from all creation
As a change from iceberg castles
Hung with snow in loops and tassels,
Christmas Island for a summer
Residence. The earliest comer
Is our own saint, non diviner,
Santa Claus. His ocean-liner
Is a sleigh that's scudding fast.
Mistletoe climbs up the mast,
And the sail, so full of caper,
Is of tissue wrapping-paper.
As he steers, he hums a carol;
But instead of fur apparel
Smudged with soot, he's spick and spandy
In white linen, dear old dandy.
With a Borealis sash on,
And a palm-leaf hat in fashion
Wreathed about with holly berry.
Welcome, Santa! Rest you merry!

Next, his chubby legs bestriding
Such a Yule-log, who comes riding

Overseas, the feast to dish up,
But—aha!—the boys' own bishop,
Good St. Nicholas! And listen!
Out of Denmark, old Jule-nissen,
Kindly goblin, bent, rheumatic,
In the milk-bowl set up attic
For this Christmas cheer, comes bobbing
Through the waves. He'll be hob-nobbing
With Knecht Clobes, Dutchman true,
Sailing in a wooden shoe.
When the sunset gold enamels
All the sea, three cloudy camels
Bear the Kings with stately paces,
Taking islands for oases,
While a star-boat brings Kriss Kringle.
Singing *Noël* as they mingle,
Drinking toasts in sunshine sherry,
How the Christmas Saints make merry!

While a gray contralto pigeon
Coos that loving is religion,
How they laugh and how they rollick,
How they fill the isle with frolic.
Up the Christmas Trees they clamber,
Lighting candles rose and amber,
Till the sudden moonbeams glisten.

Then all kneel but old Jule-nissen,
Who, a heathen elf stiff-jointed,
Doffs his night-cap, red and pointed;
For within the moon's pale luster
They behold bright figures cluster;
Their adoring eyes look on a
Silver-throned serene Madonna,
With the Christ-Child, rosy sweeting,
Smiling to their loyal greeting.
Would that on this Holy Night
We might share such blissful sight,
– We might find a fairy ferry
To that isle where saints make merry!

Santa's Stocking

KATHERINE LEE BATES

Dame Snow has been knitting all day
With needles of crystal and pearl
To make a big, beautiful stocking
For Santa, her merriest son;
And now in some wonderful way
She has hung it, by twist and by twirl,
On the tip of the moon, and sits rocking,
Old mother, her day's work done.

How long and how empty it flaps,
Like a new, white cloud in the sky!
The starts gleam above it for candles;
But who is to fill it and trim?
Dame Snow in her rocking-chair naps.
When Santa comes home by and by,
Will he find—O scandal of scandals!—
No Christmas at all for him? ...

His pack is bursting with toys;
The dollies cling round his neck;
And sleds come slithering after
As he takes the roofs at a run.
Blithe lover of girls and boys,
Bonbons he pours by the peck;
Holidays, revels, and laughter,
Feasting and frolic and fun.

Who would dram that his kind heart aches
—Heart shaped like a candied pear,
Sweet heart of our housetop rover—
For the homes where no carols resound,
For the little child that wakes
To a hearth all cold and bare,
For Santa, his white world over,
Finds Christmas doesn't go round! …

Let us bring the dear Saint from our store
Fair gifts wrapped softly in love;
Let all gentle children come flocking,
Glad children whose Christmas is sure;
Let us bring him more treasures and more,
While the star-candles glisten above,
For whatever we put in his stocking,
Santa Claus gives to the poor.

Saint Nicholas

MARIANNE MOORE

Might I, if you can find it, be given
a chameleon with tail.
that curls like a watch spring; and vertical
on the body—including the face—pale
    tiger-stripes, about seven
      (the melanin in the skin
    having been shaded from the sun by thin
      bars; the spinal dome
        beaded along the ridge
    as if it were platinum)?

    If you can find no striped chameleon,
might I have a dress or suit—
I guess you have heard of it—of *qiviut*?
And, to wear with it, a taslon shirt, the drip-dry fruit
    of research second to none,
      sewn, I hope by Excello,
      as for buttons to keep down the collar-points, no.
      The shirt could be white—

and be "worn before six,"
either in daylight or at night.

But don't give me, if I can't have the dress,
a trip to Greenland, or grim
trip to the moon. The moon should come here. Let him
make the trip down, spread on my dark floor some dim
    marvel, and if a success
      that I stoop to pick up and wear,
        I could ask nothing more. A thing yet more rare,
        though, and different,
          would be this: Hans van Marée'
      St Hubert, kneeling with head bent,

form erect—in velvet, tense with restraint—
hand hanging down; the horse, free.
Not the orginal, of course. Give me
a postcard of the scene—huntsman and divinity—
    hunt-mad Hubert startled into a saint
      by a stag with a Figure entined.
      But why tell you what you must have divined?
        Saint Nicholas, O Santa Claus,
          would it not be the most
    prized gift that ever was!

Jolly Old St. Nicholas

TRADITIONAL AMERICAN CAROL

Jolly old Saint Nicholas
Lean your ear this way!
Don't you tell a single soul
What I'm going to say;
Christmas Eve is coming soon,
Now, you dear old man,
Whisper what you'll bring to me;
Tell me if you can.

When the clock is striking twelve,
When I'm fast asleep,
Down the chimney broad and black,
With your pack you'll creep;
All the stockings you will find
Hanging in a row;
Mine will be the shortest one,
You'll be sure to know.

Santa Claus

WALTER de la MARE

On wool-soft feet he peeps and creeps,
    While in the moon-blanched snow,
Tossing their sled-belled antlered heads,
    His reindeer wait below.
Bright eyes, peaked beard, and bulging sack,
    He stays to listen, and look, because
A child lies sleeping out of sight,
    And this is Santa Claus.

"Hast thou, in Fancy, trodden where lie
Leagues of ice beneath the sky?
Where bergs, like palaces of light,
Emerald, sapphire, crystal white,
Glimmer in the polar night?
Hast thou heard in dead of dark
The mighty Sea-lion's shuddering bark?
Seen, shuffling through the crusted snow,
The blue-eyed Bears a-hunting go?

And in leagues of space o'erhead—
Radiant Aurora's glory spread?
Hast thou?" "Why?" "My child, because
    There dwells thy loved Santa Claus."

Santa Claus
Is Comin' to Town

HAVEN GILLESPIE AND J. FRED COOTS

You better watch out,
You better not cry,
Better not pout,
I'm telling you why:
Santa Claus is comin' to town.

He's making a list
And checking it twice,
Gonna find out who's naughty and nice:
Santa Claus is comin' to town.

He sees you when you're sleepin'
He knows when you're awake.
He knows if you've been bad or good,
So be good for goodness sake.

Oh! you better watch out,
You better not cry,
Better not pout,
I'm telling you why:
Santa Claus is comin' to town.

A Visit from St. Nicholas

CLEMENT C. MOORE

'Twas the night before Christmas, when all through the house
Not a creature was stirring, not even a mouse;
The stockings were hung by the chimney with care,
In hopes that St. Nicholas soon would be there.
The children were nestled all snug in their beds,
While visions of sugar-plums danced through their heads;
And mamma in her kerchief, and I in my cap,
Had just settled our brains for a long winter's nap—
When out on the lawn there arose such a clatter,
I sprang from my bed to see what was the matter.
Away to the window I flew like a flash,
Tore open the shutters and threw up the sash.
The moon on the breast of the new-fallen snow
Gave the lustre of midday to objects below;
When, what to my wondering eyes should appear,
But a miniature sleigh and eight tiny reindeer,

With a little old driver, so lively and quick,
I knew in a moment it must be St. Nick.
More rapid than eagles his coursers they came,
And he whistled, and shouted, and called them by name:
"Now, Dasher! now, Dancer! now, Prancer! and Vixen!
On, Comet! on, Cupid! on, Donder and Blitzen!
To the top of the porch! to the top of the wall!
Now dash away! dash away! dash away all!"
As dry leaves that before the wild hurricane fly,
When they meet with an obstacle, mount to the sky,
So up to the house-top the coursers they flew,
With the sleighful of toys, and St. Nicholas too.
And then in a twinkling I heard on the roof
The prancing and pawing of each little hoof.
As I drew in my head, and was turning around,
Down the chimney St. Nicholas came with a bound.
He was dressed all in fur from his head to his foor,
And his clothes were all tarnished with ashes and soot;
A bundle of toys he had flung on his back,
And he looked like a peddlar just opening his pack.
His eyes, how they twinkled! his dimples, how merry!
His cheeks were like roses, his nose like a cherry!
His droll little mouth was drawn up like a bow,
And the beard on his chin was as white as the snow.
The stump of a pipe he held tight in his teeth,

And the smoke, it encircled his head like a wreath.
He had a broad face, and little round belly
That shook, when he laughed, like a bowl full of jelly.
He was chubby and plump—a right jolly old elf;
And I laughed, when I saw him, in spite of myself.
A wink of his eye, and a twist of his head
Soon gave me to know I had nothing to dread.
He spoke not a word, but went straight to his work,
And filled all the stockings; then turned with a jerk,
And laying his finger aside of his nose,
And giving a nod, up the chimney he rose.
He sprang to his sleigh, to the team gave a whistle,
And away they all flew, like the down of a thistle,
But I heard him exclaim, ere he drove out of sight,
"Happy Christmas to all, and to all a good-night!"

The JOY of GIVING

All the Days of Christmas

PHYLLIS McGINLEY

What shall my true love
Have from me
To pleasure his Christmas
Wealthily?
The partridge has flown
From our pear tree.
Flown with our summers
Are the swans and the geese.
Milkmaids and drummers
Would leave him little peace.
I've no gold ring
And no turtle dove,
So what can I bring
To my true love?

A coat for the drizzle
Chosen at the store;

A saw and a chisel
For mending the door;
A pair of red slippers
To slip on his feet;
Three striped neckties;
Something sweet.

He shall have all
I can best afford –
No pipers piping,
No leaping lord,
But a fine fat hen
For his Christmas board;
Two pretty daughters
(Versed in the role)
To be worn like pinks
In his buttonhole;
And the tree of my heart
With its calling linnet –
My evergreen heart
And the bright bird in it.

It's Beginning to Look Like Christmas

MEREDITH WILLSON

It's beginning to look a lot like Christmas,
everywhere you go;
Take a look in the five and ten,
glistening once again,
with candy canes and silver lanes aglow.

It's beginning to look a lot like Christmas,
toys in every store.
But the prettiest sight to see
is the holly that will be
on your own front door.

A pair of hop-a-long boots
and a pistol that shoots
is the wish of Barney and Ben.
Dolls that will talk and will go for a walk
is the wish of Janice and Jen.

And Mom and Dad can hardly wait
for school to start again.

It's beginning to look a lot like Christmas,
everywhere you go;
There's a tree in the grand hotel,
one in the park as well,
the sturdy kind that doesn't mind a snow.

It's beginning to look a lot like Christmas,
soon the bells will start.
And the thing that will make them ring
is the carol that you sing
right within your heart.

Karma

EDWIN ARLINGTON ROBINSON

Christmas was in the air and all was well
With him, but for a few confusing flaws
In divers of God's images. Because
A friend of his would neither buy nor sell,
Was he to answer for the axe that fell?
He pondered; and the reason for it was,
Partly, a slowly freezing Santa Claus
Upon the corner, with his beard and bell.

Acknowledging an improvident surprise,
He magnified a fancy that he wished
The friend whom he had wrecked were here again.
Not sure of that, he found a compromise;
And from the fulness of his heart he fished
A dime for Jesus who had died for men.

Christmas Carol

PHILLIPS BROOKS

The earth has grown old with its burden of care,
  But at Christmas it always is young,
The heart of the jewel burn lustrous and fair,
And its soul full of music bursts forth on the air,
  When the song of the angels is sung.

It is coming, Old Earth, it is coming to-night!
  On the snowflakes that cover thy sod.
The feet of the Christ-child fall gentle and white,
And the voice of the Christ-child tell out with delight
  That mankind are the Children of God.

On the sad and the lonely, the wretched and poor,
  The voice of the Christ-child shall fall;
And to every blind wanderer open the door
Of hope that he dared not to dream of before,
  With a sunshine and welcome for all.

The feet of the humblest may walk in the field
    Where the feet of the Holiest trod,
This, then, is the marvel to mortals revealed
When the silvery trumpets of Christmas have pealed,
    That mankind are the children of God.

Good King Wencelas

JOHN M. NEALE

Good King Wenceslas look'd out
 On the feast of Stephen,
When the snow lay round about,
 Deep and crisp and even.
Brightly shone the moon that night,
 Though the frost was cruel,
When a poor man came in sight,
 Gathering winter fuel.

"Hither, page, and stand by me,
 If thou know'st it, telling,
Yonder peasant, who is he?
 Where and what his dwelling?"
"Sire, he lives a good league hence,
 Underneath the mountain;
Right against the forest fence,
 By Saint Agnes' fountain."

"Bring me flesh and bring me wine,
 Bring me pine-logs hither;

Thou and I will see him dine,
    When we bear them thither."
Page and monarch, forth they went,
    For they went together;
Through the rude wind's wild lament,
    And the bitter weather.

"Sire, the night is darker now,
    And the wind blows stronger;
Fails my heart, I know not how,
    I can go no longer."
"Mark my footsteps, good my page,
    Tread thou in them boldly;
Thou shalt find the winter's rage
    Freeze thy blood less coldly."

In his master's steps he trod,
    Where the snow lay dinted;
Heat was in the very sod
    Which the saint had printed.
Therefore, Christian men, be sure,
    Wealth or rank possessing,
Ye who now will bless the poor,
    Shall yourselves find blessing.

The Twelve Days of Christmas

TRADITIONAL ENGLISH CAROL

On the first day of Christmas
My true love sent to me
A partridge in a pear-tree.

On the second day of Christmas
My true love sent ot me
Two turtle-doves
And a partridge in a pear-tree.

On the third day of Christmas
My true love sent to me
Three French hens,
Two turtle-doves
And a partridge in a pear-tree.

On the fourth day of Christmas
My true love sent to me

Four colly birds,
Three French hens,
Two turtle-doves
And a partridge in a pear-tree.

On the fifth day of Christmas
My true love sent to me
Five gold rings,
Four colly birds,
Three French hens,
Two turtle-doves
And a partridge in a pear-tree.

On the sixth day of Christmas
My true love sent to me
Six geese a-laying,
Five gold rings,
Four colly birds,
Three French hens,
Two turtle-doves
And a partridge in a pear-tree.

On the seventh day of Christmas
My true love sent to me
Seven swans a-swimming,

Six geese a-laying,
Five gold rings,
Four colly birds,
Three French hens,
Two turtle-doves
And a partridge in a pear-tree.

On the eighth day of Christmas
My true love sent to me
Eight maids a-milking,
Seven swans a-swimming,
Six geese a-laying,
Five gold rings,
Four colly birds,
Three French hens,
Two turtle-doves
And a partridge in a pear-tree.

On the ninth day of Christmas
My true love sent to me
Nine ladies dancing,
Eight maids a-milking
Seven swans a-swimming
Six geese a-laying,
Five gold rings,

Four colly birds,
Three French hens,
Two turtle-doves
And a partridge in a pear-tree.

On the tenth day of Christmas
My true love sent to me
Ten lords a-leaping,
Nine ladies dancing,
Eight maids a-milking
Seven swans a-swimming
Six geese a-laying,
Five gold rings,
Four colly birds,
Three French hens,
Two turtle-doves
And a partridge in a pear-tree.

On the eleventh day of Christmas
My true love sent to me
Eleven pipers piping,
Ten lords a-leaping,
Nine ladies dancing,
Eight maids a-milking
Seven swans a-swimming

Six geese a-laying,
Five gold rings,
Four colly birds,
Three French hens,
Two turtle-doves
And a partridge in a pear-tree.

On the twelfth day of Christmas
My true love sent to me
Twelve drummers drumming,
Eleven pipers piping,
Ten lords a-leaping,
Nine ladies dancing,
Eight maids a-milking
Seven swans a-swimming
Six geese a-laying,
Five gold rings,
Four colly birds,
Three French hens,
Two turtle-doves
And a partridge in a pear-tree.

Jest 'Fore Christmas

EUGENE FIELD

Father calls me William, sister calls me Will,
Mother calls me Willie, but the fellers call me Bill!
Might glad I ain't a girl—ruther be a boy,
Without them sashes, curls, an' things that's worn by
　　　Fauntleroy!
Love to chawnk green apples an' go swimmin' in the lake—
Hate to take the castor-ile they give for belly-ache!
'Most all the time, the whole year round, there ain't no flies
　　　on me,
but jest 'fore Christmas I'm as good as I kin be!

Got a yeller dog named Sport, sic him on a cat;
First thing she knows she doesn't know where she is at!
Got a clipper sled, an' when us kids goes out to slide,
'Long comes the grocery cart, an' we all hook a ride!
But sometimes when the grocery man is worrited an' cross,
He reaches at us with his whip, an' larrups up his hoss,

An' then I laff and holler, "Oh, ye never teched me!"
But jest 'fore Christmas I'm as good as I kin be!

Gran'ma says she hopes that when I git to be a man,
I'll be a missionarer like her oldest brother, Dan,
As was et up by the cannibals that lives in Ceylon's Isle,
Where every prospeck pleases, an' only man is vile!
But Gran'ma she has never been to see a Wild West show,
Not read the Life of Daniel Boone, or else I guess she'd know
That Buff'lo Bill an' cowboys is good enough for me!
Excep' just 'fore Christmas when I'm good as I kin be!

And then old Sport he hangs around, so solemn-like an' still
His eyes they seem a'sayin': "What's the matter, little Bill?"
The old cat sneaks down off her perch an' wonders what's
        become
Of them two enemies of hern that used to make things hum!
But I am so perlite an' tend to earnestly to biz,
That mother says to father: "How improved our Willie is!"
But father, havin' been a boy hisself, suspicions me
When, jest 'fore Christma I'm as good as I kin be!

For Christmas, with its lots an' lots of candles, cakes, an' toys,
Was made, they says, for proper kids an' not for naughty boys;
So wash yer face an' bresh yer hair, an' mind yer *p*'s and *q*'s,

An' don't bust out yer pantaloons, an' don't wear out yer shoes;
Say "Yessum" to the ladies, an' "Yessir" to the men,
An' when they's company, don't pass yer plate for pie again;
But, thinkin' of the things yer'd like to see upon that tree,
Jest 'fore Christmas be as good as yer kin be!

A Friend's Greeting

EDGAR A. GUEST

I'd like to be the sort of friend that you have been to me;
I'd like to be the help that you've been always glad to be;
I'd like to mean as much to you each minute of the day
As you have meant, old friend of mine, to me along the way.

I'd like to do the big things and the splendid things for you,
To brush the gray from out your skies and leave them only blue;
I'd like to say the kindly things that I so oft have heard,
And feel that I could rouse your soul the way that mine you've
    stirred.

I'd like to give you back the joy that you have given me.
Yet that were wishing you a need I hope will never be;
I'd like to make you feel as rich as I, who travel on
Undaunted in the darkest hours with you to lean upon.

I'm wishing at this Christmas time that I could but repay
A portion of the gladness that you've strewn along my way;
And could I have one wish this year, this only would it be:
I'd like to be the sort of friend that you have been to me.

A Christmas List

MARILYN MORGAN HELLEBERG

"Ask," He said, "and you shall receive."
When you're nine years old, your heart can believe.
"Give me a doll that drinks and sleeps."
I asked, but oh, I didn't receive.

"Ask," He said, "and you shall receive."
I was young and in love, it was Christmas Eve.
"Give me the heart of that special boy."
I asked, but oh, I didn't receive.

"Ask," He said, "and you shall receive."
Money was scarce but I tried to believe.
"Give us enough for the gifts on our list."
I asked, but oh, I didn't receive.

"Ask," He said, "and you shall receive."
Sorting my values, I began to perceive.
"Give me Your Son. Let Him shine through me."
I asked, and lo, I began to receive...

More than I'd ever dared to believe—
Treasures unmeasured, blessings undreamed,
All I'd asked or hoped to achieve.
"Ask," He said, "and you shall receive."

Scrooge Rides Again
or A Christmas Poem

Backward, turn backward, O Time, you old ghoul,
Make me a child again just for one Yule;
Reverse, and if please you, the flow of the river,
Let me be a receiver instead of a giver;
Tuck me cozily into a wee trundle bed
As visions of sugarplums dance through my head,
Which would be a superior substitute for
The seasonal nightmare of yore and Dior.
Please provide for this Christmas alternative symbols

To replace Lord and Taylor, and Macy's and Gimbel's;
Christmases past are a goulash of memory,
Saksy and Schwarzy and Hammacher Schlemmery.
I can name the great musical B's without qualms,
Paying homage to Bach and Beethoven and Brahms,
It's the charge account B's that ruin my rest,
Such as Bergdorf and Bonwit, and Bendel and Best,

While hard on their heels, like a menacing zombie,
Treads the shadowy figure they call Abercrombie,
And if Tiffany's not on this roster extensive,
Well, even my nightmares don't run that expensive.
Oh, this is the gist if my annual battle logs,
If you fight off their windows, they shell you with catalogues.
The Avenue blooms like a fabulous orchid
Which wealthy collectors have called The New Yorkid,
Who, who can afford this carnivorous plant?
Though the young Aga Khan, I'm afraid that I khan't.
I will flee from Manhattan, the gay tantalizer,
No place for a glum, impecunious miser;
But what overland journeys, what overseas hops,
Will provide sanctuary from luxury shops?
When the pilot takes off, when the captain has anchor-upped,
You are already well on your way to go bankrupt.
With thrift for your armor and prudence your shield,
You race through Chicago and miss Marshall Field.
You tighten your belt and hitch up your braces
And hopefully head for the great open spaces.
But the plain where coyotes fought over the carcass
Of the obsolete Longhorn, that's now Neiman-Marcus,
Where Texans as well as inferior breeds
Go hog-wild over baubles and bangles and beads.
You conquer temptation and fly to Los Angeles,

Arriving there baubleless, beadless, and bangleless.
But here is no haven for him with a mate,
For Bullock's and Magnin's like mantrap await.
You're up and away as the jackrabbit jumps,
You reach San Francisco and bump into Gump's.
You feel doomed, like a character out of Euripides,
Perhaps you'll find peace in the simple Antipodes.
Well, in Sydney, my boy, you step out of the clouds
To the great House of Curzon, the great House of Prouds,
Which sound like tiaras and ermine and swords
And a seat in the equally great House of Lords.
Next, you lie to your wife like the naughty Pinocchio,
You deny there are pearls to be purchased in Tokyo;
You lie like Munchausen, like your own passport photo,
You blandly dismiss Mikimoto *in toto*,
And go winging to Rome, taking care on the way
To avoid Lilaram and his Son in Bombay.
Not a lira more dear than a trip to Las Vegas
Are Gucci's and Cucci's seductive bottegas.
It's Cucci for clothing and Gucci for leather,
It's a thrifty device to link them together;
Leer slyly, and hint to your wife in advance
Gucci-Cucci's a kind of provocative dance.
In Paris prolong your penurious saga
By sneaking past Hermès and Balenciaga;

You must hoard self-control to the point of redudance
To resist the temptations of London's abundance;
What with Fortnum and Mason, and Harrod's, and Liberty,
It's a pit for the feet of the flibbertigibberty,
But you hold yourself down to a tuppenny card
Of Buckingham Palace or Changing the Guard.
Then it's home again, home again, jiggety-jog,
You have outdone Magellan and Phileas Fogg,
You trot through the Customs as brisk as a pony,
With naught to declare but your own parsimony.
You've observed the round earth with deliberate strabismus,
And thus triumphed over the spirit of Christmas.
But that old human nature, though often perverse,
Is most of the time rather better than worse.
Having splintered the target at which you had aimed,
You suddenly find you're not pleased, but ashamed.
There is only one way to regain your euphoria;
Head straight for the city's most costly emporia.
Buy the stars for the grown-ups, the moon for the tots,

Buy fripperies foolish in fine carload lots,
And you'll think when the family encircles the tree,
"God has blessed every one, but especially me."

Somehow

JOHN GREENLEAF WHITTIER

Somehow not only for Christmas
But all the long year through,
The joy that you give to others
Is the joy that comes back to you.
And the more you spend in blessing
The poor and lonely and sad,
The more of your heart's possessing
Returns to make you glad.

CHRISTMAS
MEMORIES

I Remember Yule

OGDEN NASH

I guess I am just an old fogey
I guess I am headed for the last roundup, so come along little dogey.
I can remember when winter was wintery and summer was estival;
I can remember when Christmas was a family festival.
I can even remember when Christmas was an occasion for fireside
   rejoicing and general good will,

And now it is just the day that it's only X shopping days until.
What, five times a week at 8:15 p.m., do the herald angels sing?
That a small deposit now will buy you an option on a genuine
   diamond ring.
What is the message we receive with Good King Wenceslaus?
That if we rush to the corner of Ninth and Main we can get that
   pink mink housecoat very inexpenceslaus.
I know what came upon a midnight clear to our backward parents,
   but what comes to us?
A choir imploring us to Come all ye faithful and steal a 1939
   convertible at psychoneurotic prices from Grinning Gus.

Christmas is a sitting duck for sponsors, it's so commercial,
And yet so noncontroversial.
Well, you reverent sponsors redolent of frankincense and myrrh,
      come smear me with bear-grease and call me an un-American
      hellion,
This is my declaration of independence and rebellion.
This year I'm going to disconnect everything electrical in the house
      and spend the Christmas season like Tiny Tim and Mr.
      Pickwick;
You make me sickwick.

Christ Climbed Down

LAWRENCE FERLINGHETTI

Christ climbed down
from His bare Tree
this year
and ran away to where
there were no rootless Christmas trees
hung with candycanes and breakable stars

Christ climbed down
from His bare Tree
this year
and ran away to where
there were no gilded Christmas trees
and no tinsel Christmas trees
and no tinfoil Christmas trees
and no pink plastic Christmas trees
and no gold Christmas trees
and no black Christmas trees
and no powderblue Christmas trees
hung with electric candles

and encircled by tin electric trains
and clever cornball relatives

Christ climbed down
from His bare Tree
this year
and ran away to where
no intrepid Bible salesman
covered the territory
in two-tone cadillacs
and where no Sears Roebuck creches
complete with plastic babe in manger
arrived by parcel post
the babe by special delivery
and where no televised Wise Men
praised the Lord Calvert Whiskey

Christ climbed down
from His bare Tree
this year
and ran away to where
no fat handshaking stranger
in a red flannel suit
and a fake white beard
went around passing himself off
as some sort of North Pole saint

crossing the desert to Bethlehem
Pennsylvania
in a Volkswagon sled
drawn by rollicking Adirondack reindeer
with German names
and bearing sacks of Humble Gifts
from Saks Fifth Avenue
for everybody's imagined Christ child

Christ climbed down
from His bare Tree
this year
and ran away to where
no Bing Crosby carollers
groaned of a tight Christmas
and where no Radio City angels
iceskated wingless
thru a winter wonderland
into a jinglebell heaven
daily at 8:30
with Midnight Mass matinees

Christ climbed down
from His bare Tree
this year
and softly stole away into

some anonymous Mary's womb again
where in the darkest night
of everybody's anonymous soul
He awaits again
an unimaginable
and impossibly
Immaculate Reconception
the very craziest
of Second Comings

Christmas

E. HILTON YOUNG

A Boy was born at Bethlehem
 that knew the haunts of Galilee.
He wandered on Mount Lebanon,
 and learned to love each forest tree.

But I was born at Marlborough,
 and love the homely faces there;
and for all other men besides
 'tis little love I have to spare.

I should not mind to die for them,
 my own dear downs, my comrade true.
But that great heart of Bethlehem,
 he died for men he never knew.

And yet, I think, at Golgotha,
 as Jesus' eyes were closed in death,
they saw with love most passionate
 the village street of Nazareth.

Noel:
Christmas Eve, 1913

ROBERT BRIDGES

A frosty Christmas Eve
 when the stars were shining
Fared I forth alone
 where westward falls the hill,
And from many a village
 in the water'd valley
Distant music reach'd me
 peals of bells aringing:
The constellated sounds
 ran sprinkling on earth's floor
As the dark vault above
 with stars was spangled o'er.
Then sped my thoughts to keep
 that first Christmas of all
When the shepherds watching
 by their folds ere the dawn

Heard music in the fields
    and marvelling could not tell
Whether it were angels
    or the bright stars singing.
Now blessed be the tow'rs
    that crown England so fair
That stand up strong in prayer
    unto God for our souls:
Blessed be their founders
    (said I) an' our country folk
Who are ringing for Christ
    in the belfries tonight
With arms lifted to clutch
    the rattling ropes that race
Into the dark above
    and the mad romping din.

But to me heard afar
    it was starry music
Angels' song, comforting
    as the comfort of Christ
When he spake tenderly
    to his sorrowful flock:
The old words came to me
    by the riches of time

Mellow'd and transfigured
as I stood on the hill
Heark'ning in the aspect
of th'eternal silence.

Christmas in the Olden Time

SIR WALTER SCOTT

Heap on more wood !—the wind is chill ;
But let it whistle as it will,
We'll keep our Christmas merry still.
Each age has deem'd the new-born year
The fittest time for festal cheer:
Even, heathen yet, the savage Dane
At Iol more deep the mead did drain ;
High on the beach his galleys drew,
And feasted all his pirate crew ;
Then in his low and pin-built hall,
Where shields and axes deck'd the wall,
They gorged upon the halfdress'd steer;
Caroused in seas of sable beer;
While round, in brutal jest, were thrown
The half-gnaw'd rib, and marrow-bone:
Or listen'd all, in grim delight,
While Scalds yell'd out the joys of fight.

Then forth, in frenzy, would they hie,
While wildly loose their red locks fly,
And dancing round the blazing pile,
They make such barbarous mirth the while,
As best might to the mind recall
The boisterous joys of Odin's hall.

And well our Christian sires of old
Loved when the year its course had roll'd,
And brought blithe Christmas back again,
With all his hospitable train.
Domestic and religious rite
Gave honour to the holy night;
On Christmas eve the bells were rung ;
On Christmas eve the mass was sung :
That only night in all the year,
Saw the stoled priest the chalice rear.
The damsel donn'd her kirtle sheen ;
The hall was dress'd with hollygreen,
Forth to the wood did merry-men go,
To gather in the mistletoe.
Then open'd wide the Baron's hall
To vassal, tenant, serf, and all ;
Power laid his rod of rule aside,
And Ceremony doff'd his pride.
The heir, with roses in his shoes,

That night might village partner choose;
The Lord, underogating, share
The vulgar game of 'post and pair.'
All hail'd, with uncontroll'd delight,
And general voice, the happy night,
That to the cottage, as the crown,
Brought tidings of salvation down.

The fire, with well-dried logs supplied,
Went roaring up the chimney wide;
The huge hall-table's oaken face,
Scrubb'd till it shone, the day to grace,
Bore then upon its massive board
No mark to part the squire and lord.
Then was brought in the lusty brawn,
By old blue-coated serving-man;
Then the grim boar's head frown'd on high,
Crested with bays and rosemary.
Well can the green-garb'd ranger tell,
How, when, and where, the monster fell ;
What dogs before his death he tore,
And all the baiting of the boar.
The wassel round, in good brown bowls,
Garnish'd with ribbons, blithely trowls.
There the huge sirloin reek'd ; hard by
Plum-porridge stood, and Christmas pie ;

Nor fail'd old Scotland to produce,
At such high tide, her savoury goose.
Then came the merry maskers in,
And carols roar'd with blithesome din ;
If unmelodious was the song,
It was a hearty note, and strong.
Who lists may in their mumming see
Traces of ancient mystery ;
White shirts supplied the masquerade,
And smutted cheeks the visors made ;
But, O ! what maskers, richly dight,
Can boast of bosoms half so light !
England was merry England, when
Old Christmas brought his sports again.
'Twas Christmas broach'd the mightiest ale ;
'Twas Christmas told the merriest tale ;
A Christmas gambol oft could cheer
The poor man's heart through half the year.

Still linger, in our northern clime,
Some remnants of the good old time ;
And still, within our valleys here,
We hold the kindred title dear.
Even when, perchance, its far-fetch'd claim
To Southron ear sounds empty name ;
For course of blood, our proverbs deem,

Is warmer than the mountain-stream.
And thus, my Christmas still I hold
Where my great-grandsire came of old,
With amber beard, and flaxen hair,
And reverend apostolic air—
The feast and holy-tide to share,
And mix sobriety with wine,
And honest mirth with thoughts divine :
Small thought was his, in after time
E'er to be hitch'd into a rhyme.
The simple sire could only boast,
That he was loyal to his cost ;
The banish'd race of kings rever'd,
And lost his land,—but kept his beard.

White Christmas

IRVING BERLIN

The sun is shining,
The grass is green,
The orange and palm trees sway.
There's never been such a day
In Beverly Hills, L.A.
But it's December the twenty-fourth,
And I am longing to be up north.

I'm dreaming of a white Christmas
Just like the ones I used to know,
Where the treetops glisten
And children listen
To hear sleigh bells in the snow.
I'm dreaming of a white Christmas
With ev'ry Christmas card I write:
"May your days be merry and bright
And may all your Christmases be white."

Christmas Eve at Sea

JOHN MASEFIELD

A wind is rustling "south and soft,"
    Cooing a quiet country tune,
The calm sea sighs, and far aloft
    The sails are ghostly in the moon.

Unquiet ripples lisp and purr,
    A block there pipes and chirps i' the sheave,
The wheel-ropes jar, the reef-points stir
    Faintly—and it is Christmas Eve.

The hushed sea seems to hold her breath,
    And o'er the giddy, swaying spars,
Silent and excellent is Death,
    The dim blue skies are bright with stars.

Dear God—they shone in Palestine
    Like this, and yon pale moon serene
Looked down among the lowing kine
    On Mary and the Nazarene.

The angels called from deep to deep,
    The burning heavens felt the thrill,
Startling the flocks of silly sheep
    And lonely shepherds on the hill.

To-night beneath the dripping bows,
    Where flashing bubbles burst and throng,
The bow-wash murmurs and sighs and soughs
    A message from the angels' song.

The moon goes nodding down the west,
    The drowsy helmsman strikes the bell;
Rex Judaeorum natus est,
    I charge you, brothers, sing *Nowell, Nowell,*
Rex Judaeorum natus est.

The Mahogany Tree

WILLIAM MAKEPEACE THACKERAY

Christmas is here:
Winds whistle shrill,
Icy and chill,
Litte care we:
Little we fear
Weather without,
Sheltered about
The Mahogany Tree.

Once on the boughs
Birds of rare plume
Sang, in its bloom;
Night-birds are we:
Here we carouse,
Singing like them,
Perched round the stem
Of the jolly old tree.

Here let us sport,
Boys, as we sit;
Laughter and wit
Flashing so free.
Life is but short—
When we are gone.
Let them sing on,
Round the old tree.

Evenings we knew,
Happy as this:
Faces we miss,
Pleasant to see.
Kind hearts and true,
Gentle and just,
Peace to your dust!
We sing round the tree.

Care, like a dun,
Lurks at the gate:
Let the dog wait;
Happy we'll be!
Drink, every one;
Pile up the coals,
Fill the red bowls,
Round the old tree!

Drain we the cup.—
Friend, art afraid?
Spirits are laid
In the Red Sea.
Mantle it up;
Empty it yet;
Let us forget,
Round the old tree.

Sorrows, begone!
Life and its ills,
Duns and their bills,
Bid we to flee.
Come with the dawn,
Blue-devil sprite,
Leave us to-night,
Round the old tree.

The Inexhaustibility of the Subject of Christmas

LEIGH HUNT

So many things have been said of late years about Christmas, that it is supposed by some there is no saying more. Oh, they of little faith! What? Do they suppose that everything has been said that *can* be said, about any one Christmas thing?

> About beef, for instance
> About plum-pudding
> About mince-pie
> About holly
> About ivy
> About rosemary
> About mistletoe (Good God! what an immense number of things need to be said about mistletoe!)
> About Christmas Eve
> About hunt-the-slipper
> About hot cockles
> About blind-man's-bluff

About shoeing-the-wild-mare
About thread-the-needle
About he-can-do-little-that-can't-do-this
About puss-in-the-corner
About snapdragon
About forfeits
About Miss Smith
About the bell-man
About the waits
About chilblains
About carols
About the fire
About the block on it
About schoolboys
About their mothers
About Christmas boxes
About turkeys
About Hogmanay
About goose-pie
About mumming
About saluting the apple-trees
About brawn
About plum-porridge
About hobby-horse
About hoppings
About wakes

About "feed-the-dove"
About hackins
About Yule doughs
About going-a-gooding
About loaf-stealing
About julklaps (Who has exhausted that subject,
   we should like to know?)
About wad-shooting
About elder wine
About pantomimes
About cards
About New-Year's day
About gifts
About wassail
About twelfth-cake
About king and queen
About characters
About eating too much
About aldermen
About the doctor
About all being in the wrong
About charity
About all being in the right
About Faith, Hope, and Endeavour
About the Greatest Plum-pudding for the Greatest Number?

I'll Be Home for Christmas

WALTER KENT, KIM GANNON AND BUCK RAM

I'm dreaming tonight of a place I love,
even more than I usually do.
And although I know it's a long road back,
I promise you...

I'll be home for Christmas,
you can count on me.
Please have snow and mistletoe
and presents on the tree.

Christmas Eve will find me
where the lovelight gleams.
I'll be home for Christmas,
if only in my dreams.

Christmas Bells

HENRY WADSWORTH LONGFELLOW

I heard the bells on Christmas Day
Their old, familiar carols play,
    And wild and sweet
    The words repeat
Of peace on earth, good-will to men!

And thought of how, as the day had come,
The belfries of all Christendom
    Had rolled along
    The unbroken song
Of peace on earth, good-will to men!

Till, ringing, swinging on its way,
The world revolved from night to day
    A voice, a chime,
    A chant sublime
Of peace on earth, good-will to men!

Then from each black, accursed mouth
The cannon thundered in the South
    And with the sound
    The carols drowned
Of peace on earth, good-will to men!

It was as if an earthquake rent
The hearth-stones of a continent,
    And made forlorn
    The households born
Of peace on earth, good-will to men!

And in despair I bowed my head;
"There is no peace on earth," I said;
    "For hate is strong
    And mocks the song
Of peace on earth, good-will to men!"

Then pealed the bells more loud and deep,
"God is not dead; nor doth He sleep!
    The Wrong shall fail,
    The Right prevail,
With peace on earth, good-will to men!"

Christmas at Sea

ROBERT LOUIS STEVENSON

The sheets were frozen hard, and they cut the naked hand;
The deck were like a slide, where a seaman scarce could stand;
The wind was a nor'-wester, blowing squally off the sea;
And cliffs and spouting breakers were the only thing a-lee.

They heard the surf a-roaring before the break of day;
But 'twas only with the peep of light we saw how ill we lay.
We tumbled every hand on deck instanter, with a shout,
And we gave her the maintops'l, and stood by to go about.

All day we tacked and tacked between the South Head and the North;
All day we hauled the frozen sheets, and got not further forth;
All day as cold as charity, in bitter pain and dread,
For very life and nature we tacked from head to head.

We gave the South a wider berth, for there the tide-race roared;
But every tack we made we brought the North Head close aboard.
So's we saw the cliff and houses and the breakers running high,
And the coastguard in his garden, with his glass against his eye.

The frost was on the village roofs as white as ocean foam;
The good red fires were burning bright in every longshore home;
The windows sparkled clear, and the chimneys volleyed out;
And I vow we sniffed the victuals as the vessel went about.

The bells upon the church were run with a mighty jovial cheer;
For it's just that I should tell you how (of all days in the year)
This day of our adversity was blessèd Christmas morn,
And the house above the coastguard's was the house where I was born.

O well I saw the pleasant room, the pleasant faces there,
My mother's silver spectacles, my father's silver hair;
And well I saw the firelight, like a flight of homely elves,
Go dancing round the china plates that stand upon the shelves.

And well I knew the talk they had, the talk that was of me,
Of the shadow on the household and the son that went to sea;
And O the wicked fool I seemed, in every kind of way,
To be here and hauling frozen ropes on blessèd Christmas Day.

They lit the high sea-light, and the dark began to fall.
"All hand to loose topgallant sails," I heard the captain call.
"By the Lord, she'll never stand it," our first mate, Jackson, cried.
…"It's the one way or the other, Mr. Jackson," he replied.

She staggered to her bearings, but the sails were new and good,
And the ship smelt up to windward just as though she understood;
As the winter's day was ending, in the entry of the night,
We cleared the weary headland, and passed below the light.

And they heaved a mighty breath, every soul on board but me,
As they saw her nose again pointing handsome out to sea;
But all that I could think of, in the darkness and the cold,
Was just that I was leaving home and my folks were growing old.

On Going Home for Christmas

EDGAR A. GUEST

He little knew the sorrow that was in his vacant chair;
He never guessed they'd miss him, or he'd surely have been there;
He couldn't see his mother or the lump that filled her throat,
Or the tears that started falling as she read his hasty note;
And he couldn't see his father, sitting sorrowful and dumb,
Or he never would have written that he thought he couldn't come.
He little knew the gladness that his presence would have made,
And the joy it would have given, or he never would have stayed.
He didn't know how hungry had the little mother grown
Once again to see her baby and to claim him for her own.
He didn't guess the meaning of his visit Christmas Day
Or he never would have written that he couldn't get away.

He couldn't see the fading of the cheeks that once were pink,
And the silver in the tresses; and he didn't stop to think
How the years are passing swiftly, and next Christmas it might be
There would be no home to visit and no mother dear to see.

He didn't think about it—I'll not say he didn't care.
He was heedless and forgetful or he'd surely have been there.
Are you going home for Christmas? Have you written you'll be there?
Going home to kiss the mother and to show her that you care?
Going home to greet the father in a way to make him glad?
If you're not I hope there'll never come a time you'll wish you had.
Just sit down and write a letter—it will make their heartstrings hum
With a tune of perfect gladness – if you'll tell them that you'll come.

RING OUT
THE OLD
RING IN
THE NEW

Here We Come
A-Wassailing

TRADITIONAL ENGLISH CAROL

Here we come a-wassailing
Among the leave so green;
Here we come a-wand'ring,
So fair to be seen.

Love and joy come to you,
And to you your wassail too;
And God bless you and send you a Happy New Year,
And God send you a Happy New Year.

We are not daily beggars
That beg from door to door;
But we are neighbors' children,
Whom you have seen before.

Love and joy come to you,
And to you your wassail too;

And God bless you and send you a Happy New Year,
And God send you a Happy New Year.

God bless the master of this house,
Likewise the mistress too;
And all the little children,
That round the table go.

Love and joy come to you,
And to you your wassail too;
And God bless you and send you a Happy New Year,
And God send you a Happy New Year.

We have got a little purse
Of stretching leather skin;
We want a little of your money
To line it well within:

Love and joy come to you,
And to you your wassail too;
And God bless you and send you a Happy New Year,
And God send you a Happy New Year.

Bring us out a table
And spread it with a cloth;
Bring us out a mouldy cheese
And some of your Christmas loaf;

Love and joy come to you,
And to you your wassail too;
And God bless you and send you a Happy New Year,
And God send you a Happy New Year.

God bless the master of this house
Likewise the mistress too;
And all the little children
That round the table go:

Love and joy come to you,
And to you your wassail too;
And God bless you and send you a Happy New Year,
And God send you a Happy New Year.

Good master and good mistress
While you sit by the fire,
Pray think of us poor children
Who are wandering in the mire:

Love and joy come to you,
And to you your wassail too;
And God bless you and send you a Happy New Year,
And God send you a Happy New Year.

Christmas Greeting
from a Fairy to a Child

LEWIS CARROLL

Lady, dear, if Fairies may
  For a moment lay aside
Cunning tricks and elfish play,
  'Tis at happy Christmas-tide.

We have heard the children say—
  Gentle children, whom we love—
Long ago on Christmas Day,
  Came a message from above.

Still, as Christmas-tide comes round,
  They remember it again—
Echo still the joyful sound
  "Peace on earth, good-will to men!"

Yet the hearts must childlike be
  Where such heavenly guests abide;

Unto children, in their glee,
    All the year is Christmas-tide!

Thus, forgetting tricks and play
    For a moment, Lady dear,
We would with you, if we may,
    Merry Christmas, glad New Year!

We Wish You
a Merry Christmas

TRADITIONAL ENGLISH CAROL

We wish you a merry Christmas,
We wish you a merry Christmas,
We wish you a merry Christmas
and a Happy New Year!

Good tidings we bring to you and your kin.
Good tidings for Christmas
and a Happy New Year!

Oh, bring us a figgy pudding,
Oh, bring us a figgy pudding,
Oh, bring us a figgy pudding,
And a cup of good cheer.

Good tidings we bring to you and your kin.
Good tidings for Christmas
and a Happy New Year!

We won't go until we've got some,
We won't go until we've got some,
We won't go until we've got some,
So bring some out here.

Good tidings we bring to you and your kin.
Good tidings for Christmas
and a Happy New Year!

Peace

HENRY VAUGHAN

My Soul, there is a Countrie
  Far beyond the stars,
Where stands a winged Centrie
  All skilfull in the wars,
There above noise, and danger
  Sweet peace sits crown'd with smiles,
And one born in a Manger
  Commands the Beauteous files,
He is thy gracious friend,
  And (O my Soul awake!)
Did in pure love descend
  To die here for thy sake,
If thou canst get but thither,
  There growes the flowre of peace,
The Rose that cannot wither,
  They fortresse, and thy ease;
Leave then thy foolish ranges;
  For none can thee secure,
But one, who never changes,
  Thy God, thy life, thy Cure.

Auld Lang Syne

ROBERT BURNS

Should auld acquaintance be forgot
And never brought to mind?
Should auld acquaintance be forgot
And days of auld lang syne?

For auld lang syne my dear,
For auld lang syne,
We'll tak' a cup of kindness yet
For auld lang syne.

And here's a hand my trusty friend,
And gie's a hang o' thine;
We'll tak' a cup o' kindness yet
For auld lang syne.

For auld lang syne my dear,
For auld lang syne,
We'll take a cup of kindness yet
For auld lang syne.

ACKNOWLEDGMENTS

"All the Days of Christmas" by Phyllis McGinley originally published in *Good Housekeeping*. Copyright ©1958 (Renewed) by Phyllis McGinley. Reprinted by permission of Curtis Brown Ltd.

"The Boy Who Laughed at Santa Claus" by Ogden Nash originally published in *The Ladies Home Journal*. Copyright ©1937 (Renewed) by Ogden Nash. Reprinted by permission of Curtis Brown Ltd.

"Carol of the Brown King" by Langston Hughes from *The Collected Poems of Langston Hughes* edited by Arnold Rampersad with David Roessel, Associate Editor. Copyright ©1994 by the Estate of Langston Hughes. Used by permission of Alfred A. Knopf, a division of Random House, Inc.

"Christ Climbed Down" by Lawrence Ferlinghetti from *A Coney Island of the Mind*. Copyright ©1958 (Renewed) by Lawrence Ferlinghetti. Reprinted by permission of New Directions Publishing Corp.

"Christmas Laughter" by Nikki Giovanni. Copyright ©2005 by Nikki Giovanni. Reprinted with permission of the author.

"A Christmas List" by Marilyn Morgan Helleberg. Copyright ©1980 by Guideposts, Guideposts Org. Reprinted with permission from Guideposts Books. All rights reserved.

"Christmas Snowflakes" by Sasha Isabella Alexander. Copyright ©2011 by Sasha Isabella Alexander. Reprinted with permission of the author.

"The Christmas Song (Chestnuts Roasting on an Open Fire)." Music and Lyric by Mel Torme and Robert Wells. Copyright ©1946 (Renewed) EDWIN H. MORRIS & COMPANY, A Division of MPL Music Publishing, Inc. and SONY/ATV TUNES LLC Mel Torme Trust. All Rights on behalf of SONY/ATV TUNES LLC. Administered by SONY/ATV Music Publishing LLC., 8 Music Square West, Nashville, TN 37203. All Rights Reserved. Reprinted by permission of Hal Leonard Corporation and SONY/ATV Music Publishing LLC.

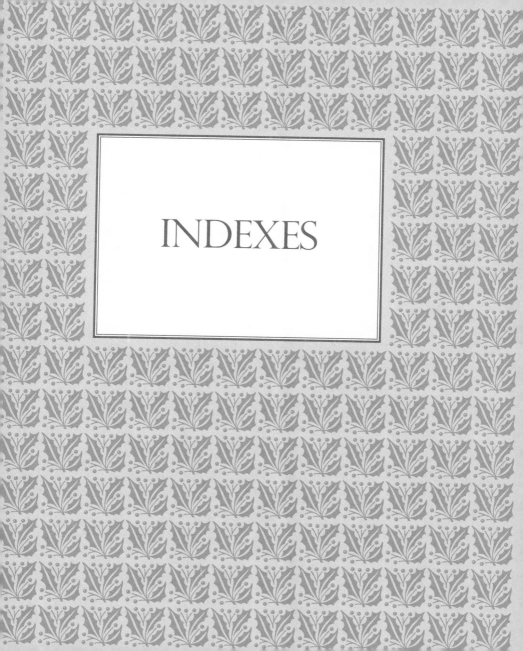

INDEXES

INDEX OF FIRST LINES

A Boy was born at Bethlehem, 275
A child this day is born, 96
A frosty Christmas eve, 276
A wind is rustling "south and soft," 285
All you that to feasting and mirth are inclined, 182
Almighty framer of the skies! 87
Angels, from The Realms of glory, 110
Angels we have heard on high, 103
As I sat under a sycamore tree, 57
As I went up the mountain-side, 61
As Joseph was a-walking, 29
As shadows cast by cloud and sun, 12
"Ask" he said, "and you shall receive," 259
Away in a manger, 108
Backward, turn backward, O Time, you old ghoul, 261
Before the paling of the stars, 81
Behold a silly tender babe, 116
But peaceful was the night, 49
Chestnuts roasting on an open fire, 173
Christ climbed down, 271
Christ was born on Christmas day, 192
Christians awake, salute the happy Morn, 155
Christmas eve, and twelve of the clock, 22
Christmas is here, 287
Christmas makes you feel emotional, 186
Christmas time is here, 169
Christmas was in the air and all was well, 245

Come, bring with a noise, 203
Come, thou long-expected Jesus, 6
Crusted with silver, gemmed with stars of light, 183
Dame Snow has been knitting, all day, 226
Dashing thro' the snow, 205
Deck the halls with boughs of holly, 164
Down with rosemary and bays, 197
Each house swept the day before, 200
Every child on earth is holy, 172
Everywhere, everywhere, Christmas tonight! 161
Fairest of morning lights appear, 114
Father calls me William, sister calls me Will, 255
Fringed with coral, floored with lava. 222
Give thanks to the baby asleep in the hay, 146
God rest you, merry gentlemen, 188
Good Christian men rejoice, 139
Good King Wenceslas look'd out, 248
Good news from heaven the angels bring, 135
Hark! The herald angels sing, 90
Haul out the holly, 180
He little knew the sorrow that was in his vacant chair, 299
Heap on more wood!—the wind is chill; 279
Here comes Santa Claus! Here comes Santa Claus! 219
Here we come a-wassailing, 303
How far is it to Bethlehem? 34
I am tired of this barn! said the colt, 36
I guess i am just an old fogey, 269
I heard the bells on Christmas Day, 294
I saw three ships come sailing in, 59
I'd like to be the sort of friend that you have been to me! 258
If Bethlehem were here today, 133
I'm dreaming tonight of a place I love, 293

In Baltimore there lived a boy, 215
In Bethlehem, 83
In the bleak mid-winter, 131
In the rush of early morning, 178
It came upon the midnight clear, 23
It's beginning to look a lot like Christmas, 243
It's the most wonderful time of the year, 158
Jolly old Saint Nicholas, 230
Joy to the world! The Lord is come, 152
Just as the moon was fading mid her misty rings, 221
Lacking samite and sable, 43
Lady, dear, if fairies may, 306
Life holds no sweeter thing than this—to teach, 137
little tree, 208
Lo, how a Rose e'er blooming, 7
Lo, now is come our joyfull'st feast! 199
Lully, lullay, thou little tiny child, 31
Make we mery, both more and lass, 171
Mary the Mother, 118
Masters in this hall, 174
Might I, if you can find it, be given a chameleon with tail, 228
My family is very small, 210
My soul there is a countrie, 310
Now have good day, now have good day! 195
O Christmas tree, O Christmas tree, 193
O come, all ye faithful, 93
O come, little children from cot and from hall, 141
O come, O come Emmanuel, 3
O holy night! 112
O little town of Bethlehem! 40
Of the three Wise Men, 64
Oh to be a snowflake, born on Christmas night, 163

On Christmas Eve I lay abed, 10
On the first day of Christmas, 250
On wool-soft feet, he peeps and creeps, 231
Once in Royal David's city, 14
Saint Stephen was a clerk, 19
Should auld acquaintance be forgot, 311
Silent Night, Holy Night! 142
So many things have been said of late years about Christmas, 290
Some say that ever 'gainst that season comes, 149
Somehow not only for Christmas, 265
Tell me what is this innumerable throng, 85
The bells ring clear as bugles note; 160
The Christ-child lay on Mary's lap, 51
The earth has grown old with its burden of care, 246
The first good joy that Mary had, 46
The first Nowell the Angel did say, 106
The holly and the ivy, 166
The little Jesus came to town; 42
The Kings of the East are riding, 66
The kings they came from out the south, 52
The other night, 170
The priceless gift of Christmas, 144
The sheets were frozen hard, and they cut the naked hand; 296
The sun is shining, 284
The thatch on the roof was as golden, 16
The time draws near the birth of Christ, 8
"Then sleep, Thou little Child." Thus, sweet and high, 138
There fared a mother driven forth, 32
This is the month, and this the happy morn, 51
Tis Christmas night! The snow, 13
Three Kings came riding from far away, 74
Twas the night before Christmas, when all through the house, 235

Villagers all, this frosty tide, 150
We sate among the stalls at Bethlehem; 105
We three kings of Orient are, 68
We wish you a merry Christmas, 308
What Child is this, who, laid to rest, 101
What shall my true love, 241
When Christ was born in Bethlehem, 71
When I was a learner, 147
When Joseph was an old man, 27
When midnight came, 38
Whence comes this rush of wings afar, 92
While shepherds watch'd their flocks by night, 99
Willie, take your little drum, 177
You better watch out, 233

INDEX OF POETS AND LYRICISTS

Alcott, Louisa May, 178

Aldrich, Thomas Bailey, 221

Alexander, Mrs. Cecil Frances, 14

Alexander, Sasha Isabella, 163

Autry, Gene, 219

Bates, Katherine Lee, 66, 222, 226

Berlin, Irving, 284

Bridges, Robert, 276

Brooks, Phillips, 40, 161, 246

Browning, Elizabeth Barrett, 105

Bryant, William Cullen, 12

Burns, Robert, 311

Byrom, John, 155

Carroll, Lewis, 306

Chatterton, Thomas, 87

Chesterton, Frances, 34

Chesterton, G.K., 16, 32, 51

Clare, John, 200

Coatsworth, Elizabeth, 36

Coots, J. Fred, 233

Croo, Robert, 31

Cullen, Countee, 83

Cummings, e.e., 208

Dalmon, Charles, 71

Dix, William Chatterton, 101

Dorrity, W.B., 172

Drinkwater, John, 10

Dwight, John Sullivan, 112

Evans, Ray, 186

Ferlinghetti, Lawrence, 271

Field, Eugene, 255

Gannon, Kim, 293

Gilder, Richard Watson, 15

Gillespie, Haven, 233

Giovanni, Nikki, 210

Grahame, Kenneth, 150

Guaraldi, Vince, 169

Guest, Edgar A., 258, 299

Haldeman, Oakley, 219

Hardy, Thomas, 22

Helleberg, Marilyn Morgan, 259

Herman, Jerry, 180

Herrick, Robert, 197, 203

Hopkins, John Henry, 68

Hughes, Langston, 64

Hunt, Leigh, 290

Kent, Walter, 293

Lazarus, Emma, 183

Livingston, Jay, 186

Longfellow, Henry Wadsworth, 74, 294

Love, Adelaide, 137

Luther, Martin, 135

Mare, Walter de la, 231

Masefield, John, 285

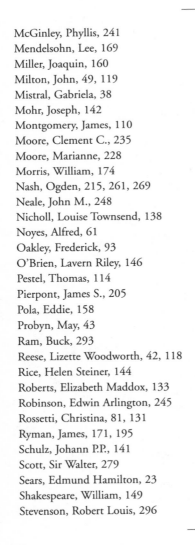

McGinley, Phyllis, 241
Mendelsohn, Lee, 169
Miller, Joaquin, 160
Milton, John, 49, 119
Mistral, Gabriela, 38
Mohr, Joseph, 142
Montgomery, James, 110
Moore, Clement C., 235
Moore, Marianne, 228
Morris, William, 174
Nash, Ogden, 215, 261, 269
Neale, John M., 248
Nicholl, Louise Townsend, 138
Noyes, Alfred, 61
Oakley, Frederick, 93
O'Brien, Lavern Riley, 146
Pestel, Thomas, 114
Pierpont, James S., 205
Pola, Eddie, 158
Probyn, May, 43
Ram, Buck, 293
Reese, Lizette Woodworth, 42, 118
Rice, Helen Steiner, 144
Roberts, Elizabeth Maddox, 133
Robinson, Edwin Arlington, 245
Rossetti, Christina, 81, 131
Ryman, James, 171, 195
Schulz, Johann P.P., 141
Scott, Sir Walter, 279
Sears, Edmund Hamilton, 23
Shakespeare, William, 149
Stevenson, Robert Louis, 296

Southwell, Robert, 116
Tabb, John Banister, 13
Tate, Nahum, 99
Teasdale, Sara, 52
Tennyson, Alfred, Lord, 8
Thackeray, William Makepeace, 287
Torme, Mel, 173
Vaughn, Henry, 310
Watts, Isaac, 152
Wells, Robert, 173
Wesley, Charles, 6, 90
Whittier, John Greenleaf, 265
Willson, Meredith, 243
Wither, George, 199
Wyle, George, 158
Young, E. Hilton, 275

INDEX OF POEMS, CAROLS, AND SONGS

"All the Days of Christmas," Phyllis McGinley, 241

"All You That to Feasting and Mirth Are Inclined," Author Unknown, 182

"Angels from the Realms of Glory," James Montgomery, 110

"Angels We Have Heard on High," Traditional French Carol, 103

"As I Sat Under a Sycamore Tree," Author Unknown, 57

"As Joseph Was A-Walking," Author Unknown, 29

"Auld Lang Syne," Robert Burns, 311

"Away In a Manger," Author Unknown, 108

"Ballad of the Epiphany," Charles Dalmon, 71

"The Barn," Elizabeth Coatsworth, 36

"Before the Paling of the Stars," Christina Rossetti, 81

"The Boy Who Laughed at Santa Claus," Ogden Nash, 215

"A Carol," Lizette Woodworth Reese, 118

"Carol of the Brown King," Langston Hughes, 64

"Carol of the Field Mice," Kenneth Grahame, 150

"Ceremonies for Candelmas," Robert Herrick, 197

"Ceremonies for Christmasse," Robert Herrick, 203

"The Cherry Tree Carol," Traditional English Carol, 27

"A Child This Day Is Born," Traditional English Carol, 96

"Choir-Boys on Christmas Eve," Louise Townsend Nicholl, 138

"Christ Climbed Down," Lawrence Ferlinghetti, 271

"Christ Was Born on Christmas Day," Traditional German Carol, 192

"Christmas," William Cullen Bryant, 12

"Christmas," E. Hilton Young, 275

"Christmas At Sea," Robert Louis Stevenson, 296

"Christmas Bells," Hendry Wadsworth Longfellow, 294

"Christmas Bells," Alfred, Lord Tennyson, 8

"A Christmas Carol," Author Unknown, 170

"A Christmas Carol," G.K. Chesterton, 51

"A Christmas Carol," Christina Rossetti, 131

"Christmas Carol," Phillips Brooks, 246

"Christmas Carol," May Probyn, 43

"Christmas Carol," Sara Teasdale, 52

"A Christmas Carol for Children," Martin Luther, 135

"Christmas Eve," John Drinkwater, 10

"Christmas Eve at Sea," John Masefield, 285

"Christmas Everywhere," Phillips Brooks, 161

"A Christmas Folk Song," Lizette Woodworth Reese, 42

"Christmas Greeting from a Fairy to a Child," Lewis Carroll, 306

"A Christmas Hymn," Richard Watson Gilder, 85

"Christmas in a Village," John Clare, 200

"Christmas in the Olden Time," Sir Walter Scott, 279

"Christmas Island," Katherine Lee Bates, 222

"Christmas Laughter," Nikki Giovanni, 210

"A Christmas List," Marilyn Morgan Helleberg, 259

"Christmas Morning," Joaquin Miller, 160

"Christmas Morning," Elizabeth Maddox Roberts, 133

"Christmas Pie," George Wither, 199

"Christmas Snowflakes," Sasha Isabella Alexander, 163

"The Christmas Song (Chestnuts Roasting on An Open Fire),"
        Mel Torme and Robert Wells, 173

"Christmas Time Is Here," Lee Mendelson and Vince Guaraldi, 169

"The Christmas Tree," Emma Lazarus, 183

"Christus Natus Est," Countee Cullen, 83

"Come, Thou Long Expected Jesus," Charles Wesley, 6

"Coventry Carol," Robert Croo, 31

"Deck The Halls," Traditional Welsh Carol, 164

"The First Nowell," Traditional English Carol, 106

"A Friends Greeting," Edgar A. Guest, 258

"The Glory of Christmas," Lavern Riley O'Brien, 146

"Go Tell It on the Mountain," Traditional African-American Spiritual, 147

"God Rest You Merry, Gentlemen," Traditional English Carol, 188

"Good Christian Men, Rejoice," Traditional German Carol, 139

"Good King Wenceslas," John M. Neale, 248

"The Hallowed Season," William Shakespeare, 149

"Hark! The Herald Angels Sing," Charles Wesley, 90

"Here Comes Santa Claus (Right Down Santa Claus Lane),"
          Gene Autry and Oakley Haldeman, 219

"Here We Come A-Wassailing," Traditional English Carol, 303

"The Holly and the Ivy," Traditional English Carol, 166

"The Holy Night," Elizabeth Barrett Browning, 105

"The House of Christmas," G.K. Chesterteon, 32

"How Far Is It To Bethlehem," Francis Chesterton, 34

"A Hymn for Christmas Day," Thomas Chatterton, 87

"Hymn for Christmas Day," John Byrom, 155

"I Am Cristmas," James Ryman, 195

"I Remember Yule," Ogden Nash, 269

"I Saw Three Ships," Author Unknown, 59

"I'll Be Home for Christmas," Kim Gannon, Walter Kent and Buck Ram, 293

"The Inexhaustibility of the Subject of Christmas," Leigh Hunt, 290

"It Came Upon the Midnight Clear," Edmond Hamilton Sears, 23

"It's Beginning to Look Like Christmas," Meredith Willson, 243

"Jest 'Fore Christmas," Eugene Field, 255

"Jingle Bells," James S. Pierpont, 205

"Jolly Old St. Nicholas," Traditional American Carol, 230

"Joy To The World," Isaac Watts, 152

"Karma," Edward Arlington Robinson, 245

"The Kings of the East," Katherine Lee Bates, 66

"Kris Kringle," Thomas Bailey Aldrich, 221

"The Light of Bethlehem," John Banister Tabb, 13

"little tree," e.e. cummings, 208

"Lo, How a Rose E'er Blooming," Traditional German Carol, 7

"The Love That Lives," W.B. Dorrity, 172

"The Mahogany Tree," William Makepeace Thackeray, 287

"Masters in This Hall," William Morris, 174

"Merry Christmas," Louisa May Alcott, 178

"The Most Wonderful Time of Year," Eddie Pola and George Wyle, 158

"Nativity," G.K. Chesterton, 16

"New Prince, New Pomp," Robert Southwell, 116

"Noel: Christmas Eve, 1913," Robert Bridges, 276

"No Sweeter Thing," Adelaide Love, 137

"Now Is the Time of Cristmas," James Ryman, 171

"O Christmas Tree," Traditional German Carol, 193

"O Come All Ye Faithful," Frederick Oakley, 93

"O Come Little Children," Johann A.P. Schulz, 141

"O Come, O Come Emmanuel," Traditional French Carol, 3

"O Holy Night," John Sullivan Dwight, 112

"O Little Town of Bethlehem," Phillips Brooks, 40

"On Going Home for Christmas," Edgar A. Guest, 299

"On The Morning of Christ's Nativity," John Milton, 119

"Once In Royal David's City," Mrs. Cecil Frances Alexander, 14

"The Oxen," Thomas Hardy, 22

"Pat-a-Pan," Traditional French Carol, 177

"Peace," Henry Vaughn, 310

"The Peaceful Night," John Milton, 49

"The Priceless Gift of Christmas," Helen Steiner Rice, 144

"Psalm for Christmas Day," Thomas Pestel, 114

"Saint Nicholas," Marianne Moore, 228

"Saint Stephen and King Herod," Author Unknown, 19

"Santa Claus," Walter de la Mare, 231

"Santa Claus Is Comin' To Town," Haven Gillespie and J. Fred Coots, 233

"Santa's Stocking," Katherine Lee Bates, 226

"Scrooge Rides Again," Ogden Nash, 261

"The Seven Joys of Mary," Traditional English Carol, 46
"Silent Night, Holy Night," Joseph Mohr, 142
"Silver Bells," Jay Livingston and Ray Evans, 186
"Somehow," John Greenleaf Whittier, 265
"The Stable," Gabriela Mistral, 38
"The Three Kings," Henry Wadsworth Longfellow, 74
"Three Kings of Orient," John Henry Hopkins, 68
"The Three Ships," Alfred Noyes, 61
"The Twelve Days of Christmas," Traditional English Carol, 250
"A Visit from St. Nicholas," Clement C. Moore, 235
"We Need a Little Christmas," Jerry Herman, 180
"We Wish You a Merry Christmas," Traditional English Carol, 308
"What Child Is This?" William Chatterton Dix, 100
"Whence Comes This Rush of Wings?" Traditional French Carol, 92
"While Shepherds Watched Their Flocks By Night," Nahum Tate, 99
"White Christmas," Irving Berlin, 284